PUFFIN BOOKS
LET'S GO TIME TRAVELLING AGAIN!

Subhadra Sen Gupta wrote over forty books for children because she thought they are the best readers in the world. She wrote about history, loved cooking up mystery, ghost and adventure stories and dreamt up comic books. She was awarded the Bal Sahitya Puraskar by the Sahitya Akademi in 2014.

Tapas Guha is an illustrator who has worked with all the leading publishers. He loves drawing comics and illustrating children's books. His vivid images have delighted children for many years. A master at recreating the past, Tapas has worked on many books about history with Subhadra.

PRAISE FOR *LET'S GO TIME TRAVELLING*

'A fascinating book with bits of almost impossible information that you will never ever find anywhere else. This book will change your opinion about history' —*The Hindu*

'Can history be fun? Well, this book certainly makes sure it is, with unique information and weird trivia about our ancient civilisations and culture . . . delightfully illustrated by Tapas Guha'—*The Indian Express*

ALSO IN PUFFIN BY SUBHADRA SEN GUPTA

Let's Go Time Travelling Again!

INDIANS THROUGH THE AGES

SUBHADRA SEN GUPTA

Illustrations by Tapas Guha

PUFFIN BOOKS

An imprint of Penguin Random House

PUFFIN BOOKS

USA | Canada | UK | Ireland | Australia
New Zealand | India | South Africa | China

Puffin Books is part of the Penguin Random House group of companies
whose addresses can be found at global.penguinrandomhouse.com

Published by Penguin Books India Pvt. Ltd
4th Floor, Capital Tower 1, MG Road,
Gurugram 122 002, Haryana, India

Penguin
Random House
India

First published in Puffin Books by Penguin Random House India 2021

ISBN 9780143447412

Typeset in Archer by Manipal Technologies Limited, Manipal
Printed at Replika Press Pvt. Ltd, India

www.penguin.co.in

Dear Readers,

Let's Go Time Travelling Again is dedicated to the memory of Subhadra Sen Gupta who lost her battle to Covid-19 on 4 May 2021.

An indomitable writer with a fantastic body of works written during her lifetime, Subhadra was every reader's favourite. Bringing refreshing, free-flowing narrative with astounding facts and dollops of wit and humour, her writing connected with readers of all ages. Capturing and integrating stories from India's rich history, this book was Subhadra's last and was in the making when the deathly virus took her away from us.

We are eternally grateful to her family for supporting the posthumous publication of this title.

Subhadra leaves behind an indelible mark, and a rich, everlasting legacy through her many best-loved works. Her books shall remain immortal. We hope for her readers to find the same magic, wisdom, humour and essential humanism that her writing echoes through this book. We believe there is no better way to remember a writer than keeping their books alive, where every page, line and word carries a piece of that writer. It is with that thought that we bring to you *Let's Go Time Travelling Again.*

Sohini Mitra
Publisher

CONTENTS

BEFORE YOU START THIS BOOK . . .

When I wrote *Let's Go Time Travelling* about the life of the people of India in the past, I had a plan. The book was going to be nothing like the history textbooks that you have to study in school. The book would have no kings or queens, no economic policy or battles. Best of all, I would ignore dates completely.

When I showed my text to the illustrator Tapas Guha, he laughed and said, 'You are being funny about history. So can I do cartoons?' We had never had so much fun doing a book together before. To our surprise, many children liked the book and have been sending me emails saying I should do another book like it. So here it is.

While the first book was about the daily lives of people, this one is about the lives of many kinds of people—all the ordinary people who have, over centuries, changed our civilization and have been forgotten. Think of the weaver who made the first loom; the sculptor who created a Chola bronze statue and most importantly, the genius mathematician who worked out our numerical system and imagined zero and infinity. Without the numbers we could not have computer programming and what is really sad is that we don't even know their names.

So, in this book, you'll read about the lives of potters and weavers; farmers and gardeners; mathematicians and astronomers; singers, dancers and merchants. You'll read also about the professions that have vanished, like the travelling minstrels and storytellers; the merchants who travelled along the Silk Road and sailors who went on dangerous voyages across the Indian Ocean. All the quiet, talented, forgotten Indians—these are their stories.

A book like this begins with all the historians whose big, fat tomes gave me all the information. Then, a book needs many friends: like my editor Sohini Mitra, who has been patiently beside me from the first book and always encourages me to dream, and Smit Zaveri, who read and reread the text and fact-checked everything to spot my mistakes. I thank them all.

Subhadra Sen Gupta
March, 2021

One

POTTERS, WEAVERS AND SWORD MAKERS

It was raining really hard and Sita had nothing to do except chat with Baba and Ma. Not that they were really interested in chatting with her.

Sita wandered through their thatched hut to the back veranda where her mother was stirring a pot of masoor dal over the open earthen fire of the *unoon* and at the same time, peeling and chopping brinjal.

'Hmm . . .' Sita peered critically into the pot with a thoughtful frown. 'Dal and begoon bhaja . . . Ma?'

'And your favourite maacher jhaal.' Her mother pointed to a small basket sitting next to the unoon. 'Fish in mustard sauce, Sita.'

Sita's smile widened as her eyes shone brightly with happiness. 'Ohh . . . we are having fish after such a long time!'

'Your baba got an order for Baluchari saris yesterday and he got the fish from the fishermen at the ghat this morning.'

'More than one sari?' Nine-year-old Sita was a weaver's daughter, so she understood the value of getting a big order.

Her ma held up three fingers. 'Three saris!'

Sita watched as her mother took the pot of dal off the fire and put a metal karahi on it. She poured mustard oil into it and opened a covered basket. Inside, there were a bunch of small river fish that she quickly cleaned and scaled. She rubbed them with salt and turmeric and then, with a loud hiss, she slid the pieces of fish into the hot oil. Soon, the air was full of the pungent aroma of frying fish.

'Oo!' Sita sprang back as the oil spit and spat up. 'The oil is too hot, Ma!'

'Go and sit with your baba and let me cook!' her mother said impatiently and very reluctantly, Sita headed inside.

Ah well . . . who wants to watch fish fry anyway? Sita wandered towards the smaller hut that was attached to their home. That was where her father had his loom and usually, she would hear the 'click!' and 'clack!' as he worked, weaving saris and dhotis, *gamchas* and turbans. It was always exciting when he got orders to weave expensive saris like a Baluchari, it did not happen very often.

As Sita entered the hut she had already begun talking, 'So, Baba, what are you doing . . . Ma was saying—'

'Quiet, Sita!' her father said sharply. 'Can't you see I'm working?' As she sat down cross-legged beside him, he looked down at her face and added gently, 'You talk too much; do you know that?'

'Of course, I do.' Sita leaned against his arm like a sleepy cat. 'What can I do? It's raining, na?'

'Very true!' agreed her Baba. 'What can you do?'

Sita bent to study what he was drawing. 'Oh! You are doing a new *naksha* for the Baluchari sari.' She breathed happily. 'What will the design be, Baba?'

Her father was sitting on the ground before a low table, bent over a sheet of paper on which he was drawing the pattern he was going to weave on the *pallav* of the sari. A Baluchari was one of the most difficult saris to weave because the pallav that would be draped across the shoulder was like a painting, there would be men riding horses, women dancing, peacocks and elephants . . . all done with threads on a loom.

'What will you draw?' Sita asked.

'You tell me. This is for the three daughters of the zamindar of Tribeni—the bride and her two younger sisters.' His fingers were moving slowly across the paper, drawing an intricate border of flowers and leaves. 'So if you were a zamindar's daughter, what would you like to wear?'

Sita rolled her eyes upwards, thinking furiously. She tapped her lips thoughtfully with a finger and then said slowly, 'I'd want a row of swans and lotus flowers . . .'

'That can even be on the border,' replied her father. He was now sketching a human figure slowly. 'We always show figures on the pallav—men, women, animals and birds . . .'

Sita curved her head to stare at him. 'Even children?'

'Sure, why not?' The design he was sketching was of a standing figure of a man wearing a turban.

'Then you can draw me!' Sita said excitedly.

His hands stilled as he turned to look at her laughing face. 'And what will you be doing? You can't dance or ride an elephant or smoke a hookah . . . those are the kinds of things I weave on the sari pallav.'

Sita frowned. 'Oh . . . I really don't know how to dance!'

'And if you smoked a hookah,' he said, grinning, 'your ma will lock you in the dark back room with the cows.'

Later, as they sat down to lunch, Baba said to Ma, 'Do you know what your daughter wants?'

'She wants to learn to weave?' Ma guessed.

'No, she wants to be in the pattern of the pallav.' The two of them laughed at her flushed face.

Sita shrugged. 'You said that girls were allowed.'

There was an odd thoughtful look in her baba's eyes as he studied her round, large-eyed face. 'Yes, I did say that, didn't I?'

A few weeks later, Sita was playing hopscotch in the sunny courtyard with her best friend Gauri when Baba called out from the hut with the loom, 'Sitaaa . . . come quick!' The two girls went running.

'What?' Sita asked breathlessly. 'What is it, Baba?'

'I just finished the pallav of the first sari. Want to see it?'

The girls crept past the long spread of the warp of cream tussar silk threads to the other end of the hut, where Baba sat weaving, his feet on the two wooden pedals that moved the loom. The crosswise weft threads were being woven in and out of the bright scarlet warp threads and he was carefully creating a painting on the pallav. The shuttle holding the spindle of threads ran in and out as his feet moved, making the loom go 'click . . . clack'.

The girls leaned forward to study the design and gasped in admiration.

'Oh, Baba!' Sita exclaimed happily. 'It is so beautiful! You have never done this pattern before.'

'Who are they?' Gauri asked, studying the two figures closely.

The pallav had a border of leaves and flowers and in the middle were two standing figures woven in scarlet thread. There was a man in a dhoti and kurta, holding a tall bow. Beside him stood a woman in a sari, holding a garland. A deer and a peacock stood by the woman.

'That...' her Baba said, pointing to the man holding the tall bow, 'is Lord Rama, the prince of Ayodhya.' And then he pointed to the woman. 'And that is you.'

'Me?' Sita raised her head, startled.

'That is Princess Sita of Mithila and she is about to garland her husband at the *swayamvara* after Rama has strung the bow.'

Sita stood there, dazzled, her hands on her cheeks, her mouth open, her eyes wide. 'That is meee?'

'Your name is Sita, isn't it, stupid?' Gauri laughed. 'So, it is you.'

Sita did a small dance around the room. 'I am on a Baluchari! I am!'

'Not really,' her Baba said, grinning. 'Right now, you are wearing a skirt and you haven't even combed your hair. The Sita on the sari is wearing a sari.' Then he drew his daughter close. 'One day, my Sita will get married and I will weave for her a Baluchari sari so beautiful they will all say, "Look, how pretty the bride is!"'

'Promise?' Sita frowned up at her Baba.

'Promise.'

~~~~~~

The Baluchari sari that Sita's father was weaving in a village in Bengal is just one small example of the amazing artistic talent of our craftspeople. In many countries, especially in the West, traditional crafts like pottery, weaving or metalware have largely vanished as most things are now made by machines in factories. In India, however, our weavers, potters, leather workers, wood and stone carvers, metal workers, jewellers and basket weavers are still creating magic by hand.

When you wander around a crafts mela and buy a pair of shoes covered in gold embroidery or choose silver earrings as delicate as filigreed moonlight, remember that a person created them by hand; they weren't made by a machine. We ordinarily forget our craftspeople, particularly those who live in villages, because they are often poor and belong to what several prejudiced people call lower castes. We must remember that they possess an artistic talent that they have preserved through many generations. So, when a shopkeeper spreads a sari shimmering with gold work before you, buy it to remember the weaver—a quiet, forgotten artist.

IT STARTS WITH A THREAD

For centuries, India and China dominated the world trade in textiles. The Chinese made silk and Indian weavers wove, embroidered and printed cottons in myriad colours and designs. Traders travelling by land along the Silk Road, which connected merchants from China and India to Europe through Afghanistan, Persia and the Middle East, and by ships voyaging on the seas carried bales of Indian cotton to lands as far as Indonesia in the east and Europe in the west. According to some scholars, the Indus River Valley was one of the first places where cotton was grown and woven. Our muslins were so popular in Rome, they were called *nebula venti* or 'woven clouds with winds'. The Mughals were even more poetic and called them *shabnam* or 'evening dew' and *abe-rawan* or 'running water'.

It all begins with the farmers plucking the white balls of raw cotton. This cotton is then spun into thread on a spinning wheel or charkha, a task usually done by women in weaver families. They hold a handful of cotton in their left hand and turn the wheel of the charkha with their right, making the spindle whirl in a way that the cotton gets twisted into thread around it. The rolls of thread are often dyed in many iridescent colours—indigo blue and grass green, turmeric yellow and lotus pink.

These threads are laid along the length of a loom and this is called the warp. Weft threads are filled into spindles and fixed into a holder called a shuttle and this is moved across and back, in and out of the warp threads with the help of two levers that the weaver moves with his feet. These weft threads, when woven crosswise into the warp threads, create cloth. So, whenever you walk past a weaver's home, you'll hear the

MA'AM, ABSOLUTELY NEW CUTTING EDGE TECHNOLOGY. HALF A SILVER COIN, ONLY FOR YOU.

'click clack' of the shuttle and you'll see a spread of designed cloth growing slowly, carefully before the weaver. It is a complex process that requires both expertise and a creative imagination. Just take any piece of woven cloth and look closely at the design of the pallav. You'll realize the dazzling beauty of an amazing craft.

What our weavers do is sheer magic. Take saris as an example—the Baluchari has paintings in thread of men, women, animals and birds woven into the pallav. In Odisha (formerly Orissa), they weave ikat, in which they first do a complicated tie and dye of the threads to create patterns in many colours. When the

dyed threads are woven, we get a sari with intricate patterns in a beautiful blend of colours. But the tie and dye of Rajasthan is a completely different process of shapes and colours. Then we have the patola of Gujarat, which has geometric designs that are dazzling in their intricacy.

Just to give you an idea of the variety of unique textiles and saris that the weavers of just one country can produce, here are a few names—mulmul, jamdani, Dhakai, Baluchari, tanchoi, Benarasi, ikat, nilambari, Pochampally, Paithani, Kota, bandhani, leheriya, Dhaniakhali, Venkatagiri, Chanderi, Gadwal, Shantipuri, Maheshwari, Kanjeevaram, garhchola, patola, Tangail, asavari, mekhela chador . . . this is just a small list, there are many more names that have a touch of poetry, each one different.

ON THE HIGHWAY

Right from the time of Mohenjo-daro, Indian handlooms and handicrafts reached markets across the world. When archaeologists were digging at historical sites in ancient Mesopotamia, they found not just Harappan seals but also bangles and necklaces that were made in places like Mohenjo-daro and Kalibangan. So, how did the black pottery of Pataliputra or the attar incense of Kanauj land up in Venice and Rome, Cambodia and China? They were carried by our adventurous merchants who were organized into guilds to manage trade efficiently. Some of the goods travelled by road and the rest by sea and our highways were as busy as they are today, except that trucks have replaced bullock carts.

There is a Buddhist Jataka story written nearly 2000 years ago that includes a list of the many kinds of craftspeople we had, and their names are similar to the Sanskrit terms for them. The book says that there were sixty kinds of crafts in India! Here are a few:

Sanskrit name	Meaning
Boonkar	Weaver
Kumhar	Potter
Yanakar	Chariot maker
Dantakar	Ivory worker
Kammar	Metalsmith
Suvarnakar	Goldsmith
Kasiyakar	Silk weaver
Palaganda	Carpenter
Suchikar	Needle maker
Nalkar	Basket weaver
Malakar	Garland maker
Silavat	Stone carver
Gandhikar	Perfumer
Chitrakar	Painter

HOW KHADI WON

At one time, Indian cottons were one of the biggest textile trades in the world. The whole world, from Rome to Indonesia, wanted our cottons. Since we did not want any of their products, we took payment in gold. During Mughal times, so much gold arrived at the ports of Gujarat that a mint was built in Surat to turn the bricks of gold into coins. Our designs influenced weavers in faraway lands. Take the famous batik designs of Indonesia that historians believe were inspired by the patterns on the cottons sent by ship of the Cholas of Tamil Nadu. The hand-block printers of Rajasthan, who were known as *chhippas*, used a mango-shaped design called *ambi* that the English adopted and named paisley. Its printing, called *chheent* here, was called chintz there. Block printed cloth from Gujarat has been found during excavations by archaeologists in Egypt. So, maybe Cleopatra liked wearing dresses made of sheer mulmul and gorgeous patolas.

When India was controlled by the East India Company of Britain, they wanted Indians to buy the textiles from their factories in Manchester. They bought raw cotton at cheap prices and taxed weavers so heavily that they could not produce cloth cheaply. Thousands of weavers were forced to work as labourers living in city slums and faced terrible poverty. Nowadays, people often criticize the Mughals, saying they ruined India. But they encouraged our handlooms and handicrafts, which helped our economy become the second largest in the world. The Mughals were Indian rulers who lived and worked in India and they spent a huge amount to support our craftspeople. It was the British who took away our wealth and burdened our craftspeople with unfair taxes and laws.

During our freedom movement, leaders like Bal Gangadhar Tilak and Mahatma Gandhi started a campaign called Swadeshi, or 'of our country'. People were told to only buy things made in India, especially handlooms and everyone in the Congress Party began to wear khadi. Pandit Nehru, all elegant in khadi achkans, and Sarojini Naidu, who swished around in gorgeous saris, made khadi trendy. As part of this campaign, people made huge piles of foreign cloth and set them on fire. Within a few months, the sale of British cotton had fallen so sharply that their factories began to close down. Once, when invited to tea with King George V at Buckingham Palace, Mahatma Gandhi went wearing a khadi dhoti, a chaddar, chappals and a huge grin, when you were supposed to wear a three-piece suit and shoes for an audience with the king. The journalists were shocked. But he gave his toothless grin and said, 'Oh, the king was wearing enough clothes for the both of us!' So, you could say Gandhiji was a fashion influencer for khadi, which went viral as the news hit the headlines.

After India became independent in 1947, the government began to revive our handlooms and handicrafts. This campaign was

OH,
THE KING WAS
WEARING ENOUGH
CLOTHES FOR THE BOTH
OF US.

led by the amazing Kamaladevi Chattopadhyay, who travelled all across the land by train, car and bullock cart looking for craftspeople who were still practising their art. In Andhra Pradesh, she found that the art of painting on cloth called kalamkari had only a few old artists left, who were then encouraged to train young artists. Today, fashion models stride down the catwalks of Paris and New York wearing clothes made of Indian textiles— zardozi and kinkhab, chikankari and Venkatagiri. And we are trending again!

MY CASTE IS ARTIST

Hindu society has always been divided by the horrible system called caste or jati. There were the Brahmins, who were the teachers, priests and advisors to kings; the Kshatriyas, who were kings, ministers and army generals; the Vaishyas were merchants and traders; and the Shudras were the craftspeople. Below them were the outcasts, the untouchables who were forced to live outside towns and villages. The upper castes of Brahmins and Kshatriyas dominated the others and never let them progress, making them labour away in their service. The craftspeople and merchants were taxed heavily to pay for the luxurious lifestyle of the kings. When a temple was built by artisans, it was the king who took all the credit. At the Brihadishwara Temple in Thanjavur, commissioned by the Chola king Raja Raja, there are inscriptions listing the temple dancers but the names of *shilpin* or carvers are not carved anywhere.

The caste system had a surprising effect, many of the Vaishyas and Shudras changed their religion. Merchants resented the way they were not given any respect in Hindu society even though they were rich and were paying taxes. In the 5th century BCE, two great religious reformers rejected the caste system, opposed the power of the Brahmins, and said that no one had to perform expensive rituals of sacrifice to pray to God. They were Gautama Buddha, who founded Buddhism, and Vardhaman Mahavira, the great teacher of the Jains— both of them were born as Kshatriyas, the warrior caste. By the way, Buddha was of royal birth too.

Thousands of merchants and craftspeople became Buddhists and Jains and they commissioned monasteries, temples and stupas, which were built by stone carvers and woodworkers. At the stupa at Sanchi in Madhya Pradesh, there is an inscription that says that the ivory workers of Vidisha have donated money for the building of the vihara. In Western countries, artists like Michelangelo and Leonardo da Vinci are celebrated, while in India, our artists have been forgotten with time—their art is not celebrated because of their caste. So, the next time you are studying a Chola sculpture or admiring the carved marble pillars at the Red Fort, think of the artists who created them.

THE WORLD'S OLDEST CRAFT

When you sit and watch a potter at work, the first thing you notice are the hands, covered in clay as they mould a small ball of wet earth over a potter's wheel. As the wheel spins, the hands shape the clay—into a curved vase or a round bowl, a lamp or a cooking pot—with swift movements. Then a thread cuts the pottery off the wheel and it is set out to dry in the sun. Later, it is fired in a kiln and decorated with carved patterns and painted designs. Every archaeological site in the world has terracotta items because pottery is probably one of the first handicrafts of the world.

All you need is earth that is kneaded into smooth clay with water and then you let your imagination take over. In the beginning, potters made long coils of clay and shaped them into jars and pots. Then the potter's wheel was invented in Mesopotamia and their work became faster. It was only later that these wheels were attached to carts to build vehicles. So, the wheels of your car were inspired by a potter's wheel and a nameless Mesopotamian potter is to be thanked for that! If you go to the National Museum in New Delhi and study the pottery of the Indus Valley Civilization, you would be astonished to find they

look very familiar—you can still buy lamps and jars in the same shapes and with identical designs at the local crafts mela.

Our pottery was valued across the world for its designs and toughness. The black ware pottery of Pataliputra in the Mauryan period, that is, the 3rd century BCE, was taken by ship to other countries. The pottery of Khurja and Alwar was called *kagzi* as it was thin as paper but also strong. A potter's creations range from a simple Diwali lamp to the exquisite idols of gods and goddesses; their art is a part of our daily lives and celebrations like weddings and festivals. In Kolkata, there is a locality called Kumartuli, where idol makers live and work. As we have many festivals dedicated to many gods and goddesses, they are always busy making idols of Durga, Saraswati, Lakshmi, Kali, Ganesha and Kartikeya, all looking lifelike and dressed in bright, brilliant colours.

The highlight of their year is the Durga Puja, which takes place every autumn in the Hindu month of Ashwin. A dazzling variety of images of the goddess are created, often with Saraswati, Lakshmi, Kartikeya and Ganesha gathered around her like a celestial family. Ma Durga stands holding ten weapons in her ten hands, riding a fierce lion as she kills the demon Mahishasura, who for some strange reason is always given green skin and a drooping moustache. For all her warrior-like looks, Durga has a charmingly gentle face, all round cheeks, large eyes and curving lips as she gazes at her devotees with a calm understanding. This image, with such an expressive face, is the creation of the potters of Kumartuli. Similarly, at the end of the monsoons, the potters of Maharashtra get busy for the ten-day festival of Ganesh Chaturthi. They make giant idols that loom over the worshippers of the elephant-headed god, happily eating modaks, clad in silks and jewellery. Only the kumhars of our country could make an elephant-face smile.

CREATED BY FIRE

Craftspeople who work with metals should really be called the first scientists of the world. They began by experimenting with iron and copper as they discovered how the ore could be melted and then shaped into pots and pans, swords and spearheads. They began to mix in other metals like tin to create alloys like bronze, brass and bell metal. Our metal workers created a metal alloy of eight metals—gold, silver, copper, lead, zinc, iron, tin and mercury—called *ashtadhatu*, and another called *panchaloha* with five metals—copper, tin, lead, silver and gold. These were considered sacred metals and were used to make idols of deities. Our metallurgy skills were so advanced that the famous 7.2-metre-tall Iron Pillar at the Qutub Complex in New Delhi, made in the 5th century CE during the time of the Guptas, has not rusted even after standing out in the open for all these years. Europe would not have this technology till the 19th century CE. The oldest metal figurine found in India is the Dancing Girl at Mohenjo-daro and it is at least 4000 years old.

In villages and cities, a blacksmith's workshop makes items of daily use like cooking pots, knives, shovels and scissors, all made on a glowing fire. Metal is softened over this forge and the now red-hot metal is shaped with a hammer. With rising smoke and a hiss, the metal is then plunged in water to cool. At one time, a blacksmith's workshop also made weapons—swords and shields, spears, helmets and chainmail for warriors. The famous Damascus swords were made of Indian steel. If you ever happen to visit the National Museum in Delhi, go and check out the Arms and Armour gallery, which has a fascinating selection of battle armaments.

One of the finest examples of the art of a metal worker are the Chola bronzes. These are images of deities, especially Shiva as Nataraja, the lord of dance. The Chola bronzes are treasured across the world and can be seen in many museums because of the delicate carving and exquisite designs of the figures. They were first made during the rule of the Chola dynasty of Tamil Nadu and the craft is still practised in places like Swamimalai. They are made by a very complicated system called the lost-wax process.

The image is first carved in wax and then covered in a clay moulding. Once the clay has dried and hardened, molten bronze is poured into the clay mould through a hole and the wax melts away. Once the metal has cooled and hardened, the clay mould is broken to reveal the image in bronze. This is finished and polished and you have the gleaming images of gods, goddesses and celestial dancers.

The lost-wax process is also used by the tribal artists of Madhya Pradesh and Chhattisgarh to make lively figurines called Dhokra. They make dancers and drum players, horses and elephants that are decorated all over with intricate patterns.

MAKING STONES DANCE

When you are walking down a corridor of any old temple, look around you at the stone pillars, reach out and touch the cool stone and run your fingers along the carvings. You'll never forget the experience. Just think of the stone carver who created such beauty out of a block of hard stone using just a hammer and chisel. You will find the finest carvings at the temples of South India, like those at Kanchipuram, Hampi and Madurai. They are alive with prancing horses, caparisoned elephants, smiling goddesses wearing jewellery and gods in elaborate crowns. Looking at them, you feel as though the granite or sandstone has come alive. Our shilpin have been doing this for about 2000 years.

We have sacred texts called Shilpa Shastras and Vastu Shastra that are like instruction manuals of architecture and sculpture. They give very precise and detailed instructions on the layout of a temple. If you study old temples, you will realize that they are laid out in an identical manner. The architect of a temple is called a *sthapati* and he heads the team of stone carvers who will create these pillared halls and gateways. The sanctuary, called the *garbhagriha*, always faces east so it can catch the first rays of the sun. Over the garbhagriha rises a spire called shikhara and the sanctum is placed within a courtyard surrounded by a pillared corridor. The larger temples, like those at Kanchipuram, Chidambaram and Srirangam, have multiple courtyards with smaller shrines that you enter through the brightly coloured gopuram gateways, pyramid-shaped structures that soar to the sky and sanctums placed at the head of the complex.

One can spend a week inside the Meenakshi Temple in Madurai just wandering around and admiring the carvings and paintings.

One of the most beautiful creations of shilpin is the monolith at Mahabalipuram in Tamil Nadu called Arjuna's Penance. A huge rock rears up on the beach with a crack in the middle and it is covered in carvings that create a portrait of our land and its people. An elephant's mother with her baby, running deer, dancers and flying apsaras, monkeys at play, sages praying ... We know this carving, which is the world's largest, was created during the reign of the Pallava king Narasimha Varman, but the names of the artists have been forgotten as they were probably not allowed to carve them within the sculpture like they would do in the West.

It is the *silavats* of Rajasthan who built the fortresses and palaces that have windows covered in filigreed screens so finely carved you would think they were like lace in stone. The sculptors of Mathura carved images of the Buddha—portraits of calm serenity as Sakyamuni sits in meditation, eyes half shut, a smile curving his lips, filling the hearts of devotees with peace.

A TWIG FOR A BRUSH

We love to paint and decorate our homes with hand-drawn motifs. Village huts have walls covered in flowers, vines, birds, women and men and sacred symbols. In the east, a paste of rice powder is used to draw intricate *alpana* patterns on the floor. In the south, the threshold of a home will often have a *kolam* design and in the north, the patterns are called rangoli. One of the most famous folk paintings are those done by the women of Madhubani in Bihar. They create their colours from natural dyes made from leaves and flowers and then use a twig to draw their dreams on the earthen walls of their homes. There are scenes from mythology and the Ramayana, everyday activities like people at work and animals, birds, flowers and mythical creatures—all painted by untrained folk artists.

The miniature paintings of Rajasthan are exactly that, but very, very small in size. The painter takes a rectangle of handmade paper, covers it with a layer of white paint and once it has dried, polishes it with a smooth stone until it gets a soft sheen. On this, he sketches the painting—maybe a woman standing by a lotus pool as a herd of deer stand by the trees. The sky is dotted with clouds and birds fly away. In the tiny painting, every detail is painted using the thinnest of brushes, from the curving eyebrows of the woman to the feathers of the birds. Some of these brushes are so thin they have just two or three strands. Then it is touched with gold and silver to make the image glow.

JINGLE, JANGLE, SHINE!

When you watch a bride walk past at her wedding, you see the glitter of her jewellery and hear the sound of clinking bangles and jangling anklets. In India, jewellery is a very important part of our lives, not just for women but also for men—just think of the necklaces, earrings and bangles that men in villages wear; then they tie a turban on their heads and are ready to party!

Many cities of the Indus Valley Civilization were centres for making jewellery and archaeologists have found beads and bangles in the ruins of many homes that were workshops. One place, called Kalibangan, seemed to have been a bangle factory—hundreds of terracotta bangles were found there. One gold necklace that was discovered had a delicate design of leaf-shaped pendants and it has such a trendy look that any fashion model today would love to wear it while swishing down a catwalk in a long dress. So, our jewellers or *sonars* were the artists of the metal world, making jewellery out of not just gold and silver but also ivory, bronze, copper, mother of pearl, thread, beads, conch shells, glass and lac and now even in plastic. Of course, if you want to keep it simple and fragrant you can just thread some flowers and leaves to adorn your neck, hair, arms and ears!

Jewellery was made for every part of the body, from the top of the head to the toes. Think of the jewellery worn by a Bharatanatyam dancer and you'll get an idea of the variety. There are hair ornaments, like the *tikki*—a pendant for the forehead—and of course a wide variety of earrings that could range from studs to danglers. Around the neck there is the short choker and then necklaces of various lengths, often with heavy pendants. The upper arms get the armlet, the wrists have heavy bracelets and thinner bangles and the fingers are decorated with rings. Around the waist, you can wear a belt made of chains and then there are anklets and toe rings.

Three items of jewellery have an interesting history. During the Mauryan period, women wore a string of chains as a garter around the upper thigh called *padapatra*. They would wear a pleated dhoti-like dress called *antariya* with a slit on the side and the padapatra would be visible as they walked. Also, you may have noticed I have not mentioned the nose ring because women probably did not wear them in ancient India. None of the books mention them and nose rings are not shown in paintings or sculptures. Another piece of jewellery that has gone out of fashion is a long bead chain that was worn crosswise over the left shoulder and under the right arm called *asianti*.

Giving names to the jewellery brought out the poet in our jewellers. For example, we have earrings called *kanchana kundala*, meaning 'tremulous earrings', a necklace with mango pendants is called *mangamalai* and the names of anklets capture their soft jingle—*manjira*, *nupura* and *kinkini*. A forehead ornament is a *sitara* or star and ivory bangles were called *hasti* after the elephant. A long necklace going down to the chest was a *lambanam* and Mughal women wore a thumb ring set called *arshi*, with a mirror in which they could check their make-up. The Bengali word for mirror is arshi, so maybe it was designed by a jeweller in Bengal. Expensive jewellery was set with precious stones like diamonds, emeralds, rubies, turquoise, pearls, amethyst, opal and coral. We also wear necklaces made of simple wooden beads and often they have a religious meaning. Vaishnavas who worship Lord Vishnu wear beads of tulsi wood and the devotees of Lord Shiva wear *rudraksha* beads and their prayer beads have 108 beads.

Jewellery is not just about adorning oneself, it is also the private property of a woman called *stridhan* and she is free to use it in any way she likes. It is given to young brides to give them some financial security after their wedding. Of course, it is also a way to show off the wealth of the family. In the Vijayanagar Empire, the fabulously rich royal women would wear so much jewellery during festival processions that their maids had to help them stand up and walk.

A potter bent over his wheel moulding river clay; the weaver dreaming up intricate patterns with just coloured threads; an image of the dancing Nataraja made in glowing metal and a delicate pair of silver earrings—our craftspeople create magic. They are the finest artists of our land.

Two

Poets, Storytellers And Bards

'Bauji, I can't see the fortress!'

'How can you? It is almost night.'

'It will be there when I wake up tomorrow morning?'

'It will be there.'

Shaukat Ali, the old Manganiyar singer, laughed at little Surjan's anxious face and exchanged an amused glance with Surjan's father, Dilram Singh Bhopa. In the caravan of entertainers, everyone found nine-year-old Surjan very funny and he did not know why. When he had a question in his curly head, he asked it. That's all.

Their caravan had begun its journey from the kingdom of Barmer, where they had entertained the guests at the wedding of the rana's daughter. When someone sang and danced for a princess, they were given a royal treatment. There was the money of course, with the guests also throwing coins at them. Bowls of delicious food were also brought from the palace kitchen for the dancers, singers, actors and storytellers. On the wedding day, they wore shiny new clothes gifted by the maharani. It had been a wonderful month for them, and after that their travels began once again.

They packed up their things in bags that were slung across the backs of the camels and began to walk again. This time it was going to be a long journey across miles of the Thar Desert, trudging up and down the sand dunes to reach the fort of Mehrangarh in the city of Jodhpur. The yearly Makar Sankranti fair would start there, below the walls of the fortress. Folk artists would sing and dance and Surjan's father would raise his voice and tell exciting stories of heroes waving swords and of pretty princesses. All through autumn, winter and spring, their caravan moved from one Rajput kingdom to another, setting up their tents in the shadow of fortress walls and open fields. There were the Kalbelias, who were dancers; the women clad in huge black and silver skirts twirled and stamped their feet to the songs sung by the men. There were the Manganiyars, men playing many musical instruments and singing such wonderful songs that the audience swayed to the tunes in delight.

Then there was Surjan's bauji, Dilram Singh, who was a Bhopa or storyteller. The Bhopas were the most popular performers of all because who can resist a story? When Surjan was born, the chief Bhopa of the family was his grandfather Sukhram, but he had died a few months ago and Dilram had taken over. So, this was the first time that he would perform at Mehrangarh. Dilram was a bit nervous and had come to talk to Shaukat Ali, the most senior Manganiyar and an old friend of his father, to get some advice.

It was the cold month of Magh and people had lit small fires on the sand dunes. The women were busy making bajra rotis dripping with ghee and thick spicy daal. The men sat chatting as they repaired their musical instruments—a flute had developed a crack and the flute player was fashioning a new one from a piece of bamboo. A drummer was polishing his double drums; a dancer sat stitching shiny buttons on her blouse.

Surjan wandered away looking for his father and found him sitting on top of a sand dune with Shaukat Ali, watching the sun go down as it turned the sky red and orange. Surjan squeezed himself between the two men, looked up at their calm, patient faces and began to ask his questions about the famous fortress of Mehrangarh that he had never seen before.

'Mehrangarh has been standing for hundreds of years,' Dilram Singh explained with a laugh. 'My grandfather performed the Pabuji ki Phad before the rana and was given a bag of silver mohurs as a reward. So, when you get up in the morning, the fortress will still be standing there.'

'Will the rana give you coins too?'

'Who knows?' Shaukat Ali sighed. 'There are other caravans with Kalbelias, Manganiyars and Bhopas at the Makar Sankranti fair. Only one caravan is invited to perform before the royal family and we don't know who will be selected.'

'My father never got the chance,' Dilram added.

Surjan screwed up his eyes trying to spot the walls of the famous fortress, but darkness came quickly and the sky above was suddenly sparkling with stars. They got up and headed back to their camp for dinner.

It was the sharp, tuneless call of a peacock that woke Surjan next morning at the crack of dawn. He lay wrapped in a thick blanket next to the ashes of the fire—nights are cold in the desert. He sat up and ran barefoot to the top of the sand dune and looked to the west and there it was—Mehrangarh!

The fortress—commissioned by the great warrior Rao Jodha in 1459—was on top of a low hill. There were arched windows with carved screens and a gateway up a narrow track winding up the hill. Then Surjan's eyes turned to the town of Jodhpur, which lay sleeping below the walls of the fort and his eyes widened in surprise.

'It is a blue city! Everything is blue!' he exclaimed.

MEHRANGARH FORT.
WOW!

The rows of low single-storey houses were all painted blue. He had seen many towns during his travels—Barmer, Jaipur, Udaipur, Bikaner . . . but he had never seen a town where all the houses were painted in the same colour. It was as if the sky had come down and painted everything. He looked up again and studied the fortress. In one corner of the fort, he could see a row of black tubes, which he realized were cannons. He had seen cannons at the Amer Fort and so he knew they were always placed along the outer walls of a fortress to protect the fort from attacking enemies.

Suddenly, Surjan wanted desperately to see the fort and watch his father perform for the rana and the royal family. He dreamt of his beloved bauji walking up to bow before the king and being given a bag of silver mohur coins.

They all arrived early at the Makar Sankranti fair and grabbed the space where their shows would take place near the gateway. Dilram Singh and his family settled in the shade of a spiky keekar tree. Dilram set up his props for the show because when he would tell the story, he would also sing and slowly unfold the *phad* on which were drawn the episodes of the story about the hero Pabuji.

As Dilram and his wife were setting up the wooden frame on which the roll of the phad was fixed, Surjan was opening the bag in which the musical instruments had been packed. There was the small dhol that his mother would play to announce that a show was about to start to gather spectators. There were the *ghungroos*, the bells that Dilram would tie around his ankles that he would jingle and jangle along with his story and songs. Then he pulled out the *kartaals*, two small pieces of flat wood that you held in the palm of your hand and moved to make them go clickety clack!

'Bauji...' Surjan began thoughtfully. 'Amma...'

His mother looked at him, crouched beside the bag and said, 'What are you doing with the kartaals? You can't play them, Surjan.'

'I can. Shaukat Chacha taught me.'

The Manganiyars played the kartaals, two pieces of wood tied with a string that they clicked with their fingers, keeping the beat to their song, their arms weaving up and down in a dance. Surjan clicked and clacked the kartaals, making his mother laugh.

'Do you want to be a Bhopa like your father or a Manganiyar like Shaukat Chacha?'

Surjan was busy mimicking a Manganiyar, waving his arms, clacking away. 'I want to be both.' This time Dilram laughed.

Noticing that his father was looking happy, Surjan wandered up and asked, 'Bauji, can I sing with you today?' Then noticing the doubtful look on his father's face, he said, 'I know all the songs you know.'

'All? Really? You know the song when Pabuji is going to fight his enemies?'

'Well, not that one...' Surjan had to admit, 'It is too long, but the first song when you describe Pabuji, that one I have learnt by heart.'

'Once we are back at our village in summer, we'll have the time and I'll teach you all the songs.'

'Please, Bauji,' Surjan begged, 'just one song...'

'No.' His father shook his head firmly. 'Not today.'

By mid-morning, the mela was in full swing. A small crowd had gathered as Surjan's amma beat the drum and then Dilram Singh began his exciting tale. As he spoke and sang, he slowly unrolled the cloth with the drawings and pointed to the pictures with a small stick. There were rows and rows showing scenes from the life of Pabuji the warrior, who

wore a tall turban, rode a horse while carrying a sword and
shield and had a thick moustache curving across his face.
As the story built up, the audience leaned forward eagerly
to watch Dilram sing and dance, wave his hands and shake
his turbaned head.

Surjan was sitting by the side, thinking, *Bauji said I am not
allowed to sing, he did not say anything about dancing.* He
reached into the bag and found half a torn string of ghungroo
bells and tied them around his right ankle. Then he picked
up the two kartaals and stood up, his heart thudding with
excitement. His parents were busy with the show, they did not
notice what he was doing.

As Dilram paused to catch his breath, Surjan launched himself
on to the space before the audience, swaying his hips, stamping
his feet to make the bells around his ankle jingle and then he
clacked the kartaals to the beat of his dancing feet. As he swayed
and swivelled his hips, bent and raised his head and began to
dance, the audience began to clap and broke into a spontaneous
'*Wah! Wah!*' in praise. Dilram and his wife watched their son
charm the audience and the smiles on their faces grew. He was
a true Bhopa after all.

Surjan moved around the spectators carrying a small bowl
and the coins kept pouring in. As he walked past a tall
moustached man, who stood leaning on his walking stick,
he did a little jig, making the man laugh and drop a handful
of coins into the bowl. Then Surjan leapt back in front of the
phad with a sharp clickety-clack-clack and Dilram went on
with the story.

The show was over. Surjan's amma counted the coins while
Surjan and his bauji carefully rolled up the phad, when a deep
voice spoke behind them.

'Bhopa, what is your name?' Dilram turned to see the tall moustached man who had been standing at the back, leaning on his stick and watching the show. He bowed low as the man looked like an important person.

'Dilram Singh Bhopa, huzoor.'

'And you are?' The man looked down at Surjan.

'Surjan Singh, son of Dilram Singh,' he replied and stamped his foot, making the ghungroos jingle. 'At your service, huzoor.'

The man laughed. 'You are a clever boy. I liked your kartaal dance.' He turned to Dilram and handed him a small metal tablet. 'Come to the fortress tomorrow morning. Show this tablet to the guards at the gate and tell them I have invited you to come.'

'Huzoor, your name?'

'I am Rao Ram Singh Rathore, personal assistant to the rana. You are to perform before the ladies of the court and bring the Manganiyars and Kalbelias of your caravan too.' Going past Surjan, he flicked a finger along Surjan's flushed cheeks. 'And you will come and dance and make the ladies laugh.'

Surjan had lost his voice and so he clacked his kartaal and did a little dance of happiness.

~~~~~~

It is the folk singers and storytellers of India who have kept our stories alive through the centuries. The travelling caravans of entertainers did not have just singers, dancers and storytellers; there were also troupes of actors, magicians, puppeteers and acrobats. They lived in villages, and often tilled the land during the summers and monsoons, when travelling on rough village roads was difficult, but as the weather cooled in autumn, they headed out to entertain people, make them laugh and cry, dance and sing along.

HISTORY IN A SONG

The Manganiyars and Bhopas of Rajasthan still sing and tell stories and through their music, keep our folk songs and stories alive. The Manganiyars, wearing white dhoti-kurtas and bright, eye-catching turbans, sit in a half circle playing drums, flutes and sarangis. In front sits the lead singer with dark kohled eyes and a droopy moustache and as he raises his voice in song, he plays the kartaals, castanets that he waves around and at the end the clickety-clickety-clack is so fast you think his fingers have vanished in a whirl of movement. It is pure magic.

The Manganiyars are Muslims, but they have preserved a part of Indian mythology by singing about Hindu gods and goddesses. Like the Bhopas, they tell stories from the Ramayana, the Mahabharata and about local heroes like Pabuji. They have also preserved our traditional musical instruments like the *dafli* (a kind of drum), *been* (flute), the seventeen-stringed *kamarcha* and the belled *khanjari*. The most interesting is a double flute called *ravanhatta* because they say that Ravana, the king of Lanka who was a great musician, invented it.

A LONG, LONG TIME AGO

Our stories have been kept alive by our storytellers—the *sutradhars*, *sutas* and *kathakars* who are the minstrels and balladeers who wandered the land carrying their bag of stories.

Even today in Chhattisgarh, the Pandavani performers, who are all women, stride around the stage playing many roles to tell the tale of the Mahabharata. The *pattachitra* paintings of Odisha are like ancient comic books and the Bhopas tell the story of a Rajasthani hero called Pabuji.

Traditionally, the sutas were the sons of Kshatriyas and lower-caste women. They could not become warriors, but they worked in the palaces and often became charioteers. In the Mahabharata, many important characters are sutas. Dhritarashtra and Pandu's half-brother Vidur was a suta because his mother was a maid. Karna, though a Kshatriya, was brought up by a charioteer, and was always called a *sutaputra*. Sanjaya, Dhritarashtra's charioteer becomes a narrator of the events on the battlefield at Kurukshetra. The most interesting suta is a king who chooses to become a charioteer when Krishna, the ruler of Dwarka, drives his friend Arjuna's chariot on the battlefield.

The biggest warriors were called *maharathis* as they fought from chariots called *rathas*. In the battlefield, the charioteer's skills in driving the horses was a crucial factor in the fighting and at Kurukshetra, Krishna saved Arjuna's life more than once. So, the sutas watched the battle first-hand and once the battle was over, they would begin their travels through the kingdom, narrating a blow-by-blow account of the battle. Then, to make the story more exciting, they would add tales of gods and demons, add magical weapons like the *astras* of the epics, add a ghost here, a weeping woman there and then they would sing and dance. It was always a great show and this is one reason why our films have heroes and heroines who sing and dance—our actors from Rajnikanth to Deepika Padukone are all modern sutradhars.

It is said that Ved Vyasa collected all the stories and wrote them down and his student Vaisampayana learnt the verses of the Mahabharata from him. Vaisampayana narrated these at a *yagya* before King Janamejaya, who was the great-grandson of Arjuna. Here it was heard by a suta named Romaharsana, who taught it to his son Ugrasravas and they carried the epic tale across the land. The names of the two sutas are really very interesting—Romaharsana means 'his stories will make your hair stand up' and Ugrasravas means 'a storyteller with a very loud voice'.

Originally the story of the battle, as written by Ved Vyasa, was called 'Jaya' and as it spread across the land, some sutas added more stories, philosophers put in their lectures like the Gita, other sutas added travel stories, astrological predictions, folk tales and a lot of priestly mumbo jumbo, until it had grown beyond the battle and become the longest poem in the world

with one lakh verses. This is the work of hundreds of sutas, priests and philosophers and this giant compilation began to be called the Mahabharata.

There were many versions of the epic in regional languages. Now there are so many Mahabharatas, often telling different stories, that the Bhandarkar Oriental Research Institute in Pune is studying the many volumes as part of its Mahabharata Project.

THE SONGS OF THE RIG VEDA

The Aryans were nomadic tribes that moved from Central Asia to Persia and then across Afghanistan. They entered the Indian subcontinent around 1500 BCE through the Himalayan passes in the north-west like the Khyber Pass. Being nomads meant their wealth was in their cattle and they wandered the land looking for meadows of grass. Unlike the people of the Indus Valley Civilization, they did not settle in villages or build cities for nearly a thousand years.

Imagine the life of the Aryans, wandering around in forests full of wild animals, beside rivers and hills, watching the sun rise and the moon and stars come out at night. So, their first gods and goddesses were these aspects of nature—Surya, the sun god; Agni, the god of fire; Indra, who brought rain; and Ushas, the goddess of dawn. The poets among the herdsmen composed poetry in praise of these gods and goddesses and they would sing these hymns when they prayed around a sacred fire—this religious ritual came to be called yagya. Their songs have survived in the ancient book called the Rig Veda.

The Rig Veda is one of the oldest religious texts in the world and is said to have been composed between 1500 BCE and

900 BCE. The 1028 hymns of the Rig Veda are the work of wandering herdsmen and women—they show real talent. Three other Vedas would follow—the Sam Veda has hymns rearranged so that it could be used by priests during their chanting. The Yajur Veda is a mix of verses and prose and gives the many rules of rituals during a yagya that included animal sacrifice. The Atharva Veda has magical spells and incantations in verse. So, we have spells against illness or snake bite, prayers for the welfare of children and good health and even a few curses!

These poets wrote verses that were full of images of nature, feelings and beauty. Here is a poem dedicated to Aranyani, the goddess of the forest, that reads like a love song.

'Lady of the forest! Lady of the forest!
Who seems to vanish from sight in the distance,
Why do you never come to the village?
Surely you are not afraid of men!'

(Translated by A.L. Basham)

The poets of the Rig Veda came to be called rishis and not all of them were male Brahmins. Rishi Vishwamitra was a Kshatriya and the poets Gargi and Maitreyi were women. Many hymns were not religious. There is one called the 'Gamester's Lament' which is a prayer by a gambler wishing that the dice would fall to help him win some money! After the four Vedas, other books followed and often they were commentaries on the Vedas and philosophical thoughts of scholars, called the Brahmanas, Aryanakas and Upanishads. They were all written by poets and philosophers who were given the title of rishi. Then there were the Puranas, which are a mix of history and mythological stories of deities and it is these mythological tales that we have grown up with. By the time the Puranas were written, the Aryans had moved across Punjab and spread across the banks of the Ganga River, settled down in villages and towns and stopped their wanderings.

What is astonishing is that in the early years, the Rig Veda was not written down. Unlike the people of the Indus Valley Civilization, the Aryans had no script. Instead, the verses were memorized by the priests and taught to the young— father to son; teacher to student. The verses were memorized by endless repetition and they had to be very careful about the correct pronunciation of the Sanskrit words. This oral tradition was a mammoth exercise, and the words were pronounced the same way across the land. However, over the years, some of the words became obscure as people forgot their meaning and today, at times, the Rig Veda is very hard to understand.

We have no idea when the Sanskrit alphabet was developed, but gradually the books were written down. This alphabet, many scholars like the historian A.L. Basham think, is the most organized and logical form among all the alphabets in the world. For example, all the vowels come first and then all the variations of a consonant or sound like 'ka' or 'da' are placed together and classified carefully. Then in the 4th century BCE the grammarian Panini wrote the *Ashtadhyayi*, in which he laid down the rules of Sanskrit grammar and so Sanskrit has not changed at all in thousands of years.

YOU SPEAK, I'LL WRITE

The oldest script found in India is the lines of mysterious symbols on the seals of the Indus Valley Civilization. Sadly, even after 5000 years and the use of computers, no one has been able to decipher it. The earliest Indian writings that we can read are the edicts of the Mauryan emperor Ashoka, who had them carved on stone pillars and rocks. This script is called Brahmi and it was deciphered by James Prinsep in the 19th century CE. Suddenly, this long-forgotten king was talking to us again about his thoughts and beliefs. Sanskrit, one of the oldest Indian languages, resembles the Indo-European family of languages, which includes Persian, Greek and Latin. By the time of the Mauryans, people were using simpler versions called Pali, Prakrit and Apabhramsa and a basic script may have been in use long before the Ashokan edicts.

Most regional languages like Bengali, Marathi or Kannada are linked to one of the two mother languages—Sanskrit and Tamil. Languages change over time and the Sanskrit of the poetry of Kalidas of the 7th century CE is very different from the hymns of the Rig Veda. When we started writing there was no paper; we used the *talpatra*, the leaves of the palmyra palm and the bark of birch trees. The leaves were cut and smoothened and text was inscribed on them using a stylus—a pointed pen. Then the pages were smeared with powdered charcoal mixed with vegetable juice, which revealed the words. In later years, an ink was made from lampblack and used by scribes. The leaf manuscripts crumbled easily and had to be preserved very carefully against insects, damp, dust and fire. Two holes were made on one side and tied with string and two wooden pieces placed on the top and bottom as covers and the whole packet would be wrapped up in cloth. Then, when the pages began to crumble, a scribe would copy them out again on to new palm leaves. It was a very time-consuming process and many books just vanished because no one bothered to copy them out. But you can find these bundles on the shelves of manuscript libraries even today.

Paper, made from bamboo in China as early as the 2nd century BCE and brought to India by traders, was very expensive in the beginning. Another reason that paper books came late to India was because Brahmin priests wanted to hold on to all the knowledge and hence discouraged the printing of books. They declared that the Vedas were sacred and could not be read by anyone except the priests. Paper began to be used by the time the Muslims and the sultans ruling in Delhi in the 13th century arrived, but we still did not know how to print a book. Each book had to be written by hand by a calligrapher and the manuscripts had painted borders and even miniature paintings as illustrations. Some of the most beautiful manuscripts were produced in the *karkhana* of painters set up by the Mughal emperor Akbar at Fatehpur Sikri in the 16th century CE. He even got the Mahabharata translated into Persian and the book is full of scenes from the royal court, battles and hunting.

What is puzzling is how printing came so late to India. The Chinese had invented woodblock printing and printing

machines were invented in Europe after. This meant that hundreds of copies of a book could be printed to spread knowledge to people and make people literate. But the education of people was never a priority of the kings and as the priests had a monopoly over education, they refused to share their knowledge with the other castes. The absence of books meant that we fell behind the West in science, medicine and technology. It was only with the arrival of the English that books began to be printed not only in English but also in Indian languages.

LISTEN AND REMEMBER

Veda means knowledge and our scholars mention two kinds of literature—*shruti* and *smriti*. The Vedas are called shruti or 'heard'—it is believed that the text was revealed to the rishis while they were meditating. The shrutis are believed to be communication from the gods and so they cannot be changed. That is one of the reasons that priests became so obsessed with pronouncing the mantras perfectly.

What the people understood and loved was the literature called smriti or 'words that were remembered'. In the smriti are the hundreds of mythological tales from the Puranas, the technical manuals called shastras like the Natya Shastra about dance and music and the Vastu Shastra on architecture. The finest smritis are of course the two magnificent epics, the Ramayana and the Mahabharata. The epics are also called *itihasa* or 'history' and if you read them carefully, you can discover how people lived in the past. For example, if you are interested in food, like most of us are, you can read that the Pandava brothers, of the Mahabharata, had a picnic by the banks of the Yamuna River and ate roasted meats. For a dancer, the Natya Shastra explains the mudras of dance. If you enjoy travelling, you can follow the journey of Rama across the land in the Ramayana. The smritis are enjoyed even today, but sadly the Vedas that the priesthood refused to share have been forgotten.

The word *purana* means 'old' or 'ancient stories' and they are a fascinating mishmash of legends, lists of kings, mythology and religious instructions. They are a record of the creative imagination of our writers as they wove stories around our gods and goddesses, who are the heroes, and the asuras and rakshasas, who are the villains. We get the story of Durga killing Mahishasura and Shiva destroying the three cities of asuras with one arrow. We had a strange tradition in which a book rarely gave the name of the author or any proper dates and was usually credited to gods like Vayu, Agni or Vishnu and we have books titled Vishnu Purana, Bhagavat Purana or Shiv Purana.

There are spicy stories, pilgrimages are described and we get geographical locations of the places, mountains and rivers. The only thing missing is advertisements! The Pandava brothers are

said to have done a circuit of all the important pilgrimages and the landscape of the country, from Kashmir to Kerala, is described, showing that we had quite a good geographical knowledge of our land. For example, Rama started his journey in Ayodhya in Uttar Pradesh, arrived at Rameswaram in Tamil Nadu and then crossed the sea to enter Sri Lanka. Do remember this was a time when people just walked or used bullock carts.

A VERY POETIC MEETING

A sangam is a meeting or a gathering, and the oldest Tamil literature is called Sangam literature because it is traced back to three great literary gatherings of poets that probably took place during the reign of the Pandya kings. The sangams were held in Madurai in the early centuries of the Christian era, when wandering poets, bards and minstrels from all over the kingdom were invited to present their work before a gathering of royalty and scholars. Eight anthologies were collected between the 3rd and 5th centuries CE with 2279 poems that varied in length from 3 to 800 lines. There were 473 poets, including thirty women and 102 who remain anonymous. It is a majestic collection that was edited and the name of the poet and the occasion of the composition are mentioned at the end of every poem.

Indians like tall tales and so it was claimed that there were three sangams that lasted for over 9900 years; the first of 4400 years; the second of 3700 years and the third of 1850 years! Even a few gods are included among the 8598 poets and 197 Pandya dynasty kings! We could probably take out a few zeroes to get a more sensible number. Although according to some scholars, it is the work of four or five generations of poets over approximately

150 years. What makes it amazing is that something that was created two millennia ago has been preserved so well.

What makes Sangam literature much more enjoyable than Sanskrit is that it is less about praying to the gods or praising kings and more about the life of the people. There are two main themes—*akam* or 'love' and *puram* or 'war'. Friendships, festivals, harvests and cooking are also explored. Here is a poem describing a young bride who has been slaving in the kitchen:

> 'My garments smell of ghee and curry
> And is stained with dirt and lamp black'

> (Translated by A.L. Basham)

Instead of the hymns saying, 'O powerful god! Listen to my prayer!' as they do in the Rig Veda; it is the voice of ordinary people that one enjoys reading. For instance, like the Gamester's Lament in the Rig Veda, here is a prayer of a melon thief and a very interesting conversation with the moon:

> 'Bright moon, I beg you not to come out,
> Wait where you are till I have cut these melons.
> But when I have got my melons safely away,
> Then come out or not, just as you please.'

> (Translated by A.L. Basham)

Tamil's greatest compositions are two long poems—*Cilappatikaram*, 'The Jewelled Anklet' by Ilango Adigal and *Manimekhalai*, 'The Jewelled Belt' by Sattanar, both of which feature strong female characters. In *Silappadigaram*, the heroine, Kannaki, fights to get justice for her husband, Kovalan,

BRIGHT MOON, I BEG YOU NOT TO COME OUT,
WAIT WHERE YOU ARE TILL I HAVE CUT THESE MELONS.
BUT WHEN I HAVE GOT MY MELONS SAFELY AWAY,
THEN COME OUT OR NOT, JUST AS YOU PLEASE

when he is wrongly accused of stealing the queen's anklet and executed. In *Manimekhalai*, the heroine wants to become a Buddhist nun. Both books have delightful descriptions of life in villages and cities. Then there is Kamban's Ramayana, which is a lively retelling of the Valmiki epic. Like Panini's grammar, the first text on Tamil grammar is *Tolkappiyam*, and there is the majestic *Thirukkural* written by Thiruvalluvar in the 13th century CE with short verses on topics ranging from morality to love and war.

Right from the time of the Pallavas, literature was patronized by kings and some of them were poets and writers themselves, like the Pallava king Mahendravarman, who wrote humorous plays and Krishnadevaraya of Vijayanagar, who was a serious poet.

A PEOPLE'S SONG

As you may have realized by now, our literature is not just the creation of scholarly priests. It is also the voice of the people—often illiterate, poor and powerless. Even then they spoke up through their poetry against the injustices of society and created a movement that ultimately changed Hindu society and worship. It was the opposite of the Vedas and we call it Bhakti. Bhakti means 'devotion'.

Bhakti poets were interested in adoring their favourite deity and not in expensive religious rituals and the presence of priests. Among the Bhakti poets were a boatman, a cobbler, a smart housemaid, a Mughal nobleman, a Rajput princess and a very unusual weaver. And we still remember their songs though the songs of the Vedas have been forgotten. The dohas of Kabir, the verses of Basavanna, Andal and Mirabai are part of our lives. Unlike the impossible to understand Sanskrit of the Vedas, Bhakti poetry is in our spoken tongues and sung everywhere.

The Bhakti movement began in Tamil Nadu around 6th century CE and we would have one of the greatest Bhakti poets, Guru Nanak, in the region of Punjab in the 16th century CE, a thousand years later. It was not just about poetry and song, it was a social revolution. Its message was simple: the Supreme Deity, whatever you want to call him or her, Shiva or Vishnu or the Devi, belongs to all of us and not just to the upper castes. In the eyes of our gods, we are equal and they are willing to listen to our prayers without the need for expensive rituals. All you need to pray is a handful of flowers, maybe a lamp and you can speak directly to God. You do not have to chant Sanskrit mantras, pour ghee into a fire, sacrifice animals or pay a Brahmin for the rituals.

The Tamil poets who sing in praise of Shiva are called Nayanars and the poets who worship Vishnu are called Alvars. They speak to God directly with love and devotion as if the deity is their friend, not some ferocious god living in the sky like Agni or Indra. As the poet Apparswami sang:

'You are father, you are mother.
You are elder brother.
You are all kinsmen.'

Bhakti changed the way we prayed and it led to changes in our society as the work of the poets entered temples and were sung before the deity. Gurdwaras not only preserve the

I'M GOD'S SOLE AGENT ON EARTH. AND HERE'S MY APPOINTMENT LETTER SIGNED BY GOD HIMSELF.

poetry of Guru Nanak, but also of Kabir and other Bhakti poets in the sacred book, the Guru Granth Sahib. The poetess Andal's songs are sung at weddings and in Maharashtra, people go dancing and singing the verses of Tukaram to the Lord Vitthala Temple in Pandharpur. Bhakti is also a protest movement as the poets point out the inequality in Indian society. Ravidas was a Dalit cobbler who was forced to live outside Varanasi. So, he protested against the disgusting caste system by criticizing it through his poetry. Basavanna denied the rules of the caste system and no one even knew the religion or caste of Kabir as he laughed at both Brahmin priests and Muslim mullahs and their silly superstitions.

It is a miracle that Bhakti spread across the land. Remember this is a time when there were no telephones, postal service, email, telegraphs or internet. So who carried the Bhakti songs through villages and cities? Our sutradhars, of course! Singing and dancing and telling stories and as they were also lower caste, they were leading a revolution with passion and love.

One day, Bhakti's message of religious tolerance and equality would reach the court of the Mughal emperor Akbar and one of his senior ministers, Abdur Rahim Khan-i-Khanan, a Muslim nobleman, would write verses in praise of Lord Krishna as 'Rahim'. A Rajput princess Mirabai would abandon her royal life and wander the land singing of her love for Krishna and one of our greatest singers, M.S. Subbalakshmi would go on to sing her songs. When Tulsidas took the Sanskrit Ramayana and wrote the *Ramcharitmanas* in Awadhi, everyone could read the Ramayana and even today devotees read a few pages every day.

Guru Nanak wandered around the land with his companion, the Muslim rabab player Mardana and he laid the foundation of a new religion—Sikhism. For Nanak, everyone was equal. He rejected the caste system and began the generous system of

HE'S A BHAKTI SINGER.
HE IS SINGING
ABOUT RELIGIOUS
TOLERANCE AND
EQUALITY.

HE'LL GET
ARRESTED
FOR
SEDITION!

langar, where everyone first prayed together before the Guru
Granth Sahib and then they cooked and ate a meal together.
Bhakti was also the voice of women and many of them became
wandering ascetics like Akka Mahadevi of Tamil Nadu and Lal
Ded of Kashmir. The Marathi Varkari poets include women like
Bahinabai, Janabai, Muktabai and Soyarabai. Janabai worked
in people's houses and she treated Lord Vitthala as a friend. She

had a sense of humour and asked her special friend to help her with the housework too.

The Bhakti poets wrote verses of sensitive power and passion and they are not just religious hymns—they are poetry of a very high order. Here is a poem by Tukaram, the greatest of the Marathi Varkari poets:

'Whirl around yourself
And the world seems to whirl around you.
Stand still and everything is stilled.
Within a vast stillness, yell. And echoes will ring.
Says Tuka
When clouds race, the moon seems to run.'

(Translated by Dilip Chitre)

On a rainy, windy night, go out and look up at the clouds racing across the sky and you'll understand what Tukaram was describing. The moon does seem to run.

Three

ASTRONOMERS, MATHEMATICIANS AND DOCTORS

Durga stood looking up at the laburnum tree, carefully studying the golden flowers drooping down like . . . She frowned for a moment and then said to herself, 'Like Amma's long earrings.' She gave a little shrug of delight at the idea. 'Amaltas jhumkas! If I had them, I would move my head this way and that way and make them sway.'

Nagasena, busy grinding dried herbs in a small marble mortar and pestle, looked up and laughed at his nine-year-old daughter. 'I asked you to get me the amaltas pods, not dream of earrings.' Obediently, Durga jumped up to grab the low-hanging branch of the laburnum tree and pluck a couple of pods. She dropped them next to her father and said, 'Here you are, Baba.'

'What am I going to do with the pods?' As always Nagasena began asking questions about his healing medicines.

'First dry them,' she replied quickly, 'then grind them into powder.'

'And what will the powder do?'

'Heal boils on the skin ...' Durga was skipping away. 'You are asking questions again.'

'If I don't ask questions, how will you learn?'

'I don't want to learn.' Durga gave a stubborn shake of her head. 'It is so hard to remember, there are so many herbs and leaves and seeds and pods ...'

'I thought you liked herbs and trees and flowers and fruits ...' An amused smile curved Nagasena's lips. 'You were telling your amma you are nature's daughter and so you don't want to learn to cook. And you don't want to learn about making medicines either, then what do you want to do?'

Just then they heard the clang of a stick hitting metal and the call 'Bhikshu Aditya is here!' Durga breathed in relief and ran busily towards the kitchen. 'I have to get the rice, Baba ...' She thought to herself, *Uff! The bhikshu saved me from another of Baba's lectures!*

Durga lived in the famous city of Pataliputra and her father, Nagasena, was an Ayurvedic doctor or vaid. Their tiny home with a red tiled roof had a big herb garden at the back, where he grew all the herbs that he needed for his medicines—amla, ashvagandha, mulethi and tulsi, Durga knew all the names. When patients came, he would examine them carefully, ask many questions and then prescribe a medicine that he would make himself. There were powders wrapped in leaf packets and

liquids in small earthen jars stacked in the clinic. The amaltas bloomed in the courtyard in the beginning of summer and he was getting his potions ready for boils, fevers and stomach aches.

King Ashoka of the Mauryan dynasty had commissioned a Buddhist vihara nearby and many young monks who lived in the monastery went begging for food from all the homes in their locality. That is how Durga had met Bhikshu Aditya. She had heard the sound of his bell and had run to the door to find a tall, thin young man clad in saffron robes with a shaven head, standing there with a smile. Her amma had hurried out with rice, lentils and vegetables and poured them into his begging bowl. Durga looked forward to Aditya's arrival every morning and now she skipped up to him holding a basket of vegetables picked from their kitchen garden.

'I have spinach, gourd and pumpkin ...'

'Oh, thank you, Durga!' As he put the vegetables in his cloth shoulder bag, Adita asked, 'Is your father home?'

'Yes, he is.' She waved towards the back veranda.

'Is he busy?'

'Not really. He is grinding medicines and as always ...' she said with a gusty sigh, 'he is asking me really difficult questions.'

Aditya walked into the house. 'What kind of questions?'

'Oh, you know. If your patient has backache, what oil would help relieve their pain? What is better for a cough, mulethi or ginger and honey? Today it is all about the amaltas ...' She gave a mock frown. 'He never stops!'

Aditya laughed. 'Your father is a great teacher and you are lucky. Most teachers would refuse to have a girl as a student.'

Nagasena, who was busy pouring some ground powder into a jar, looked up with a smile. 'Aditya! I hope Durga has given you something good this morning.'

Aditya sat down before the vaid. 'She gives me more than I deserve.' He paused. 'Vaidji, I have come to you with a request from the head of our monastery. I hope you will not refuse me.'

'Of course. Tell me.'

'Will you teach me Ayurveda? We are now nearly forty monks at the vihara and there should be a monk who knows about medicines. I want to become your student and learn how to heal sick people.' He paused again. 'The most senior monk at the vihara, Prior Adiratha, has agreed to my coming here every day and he has promised to pay whatever your teaching fees are ...'

Nagasena smiled. 'I'll be happy to teach you, Bhikshu, but I don't take money for sharing my knowledge of medicine.'

'You will be my guru and gurus are given a guru dakshina,' Aditya protested. 'You cannot refuse.'

'Well, there is something...' Nagasena said slowly. 'I hear your vihara has a wonderful library... I would like to read there.'

'Of course! The library is for everyone.'

Durga who had been listening now spoke, 'You have a student, Baba. Does that mean you will stop teaching me?'

'Of course not! Now I have two students, that's all.'

Durga curved her neck with a begging smile. 'But I don't mind at all, Baba! You teach the bhikshu while I . . .'

'Play in the garden, chat with the goats, wear garlands . . .' Nagasena shook his head. 'You will learn too. Tomorrow, we start with the names of herbs and aromatics.'

'Oh, I know! Bhringaraj and amla, haldi and dhania.' She gave a dramatic sigh. 'It is quite easy, Bhikshu. I know them all already!'

'Oh, do you?' Nagasena pulled out a brown leaf from a bag. 'What is this?'

'Mmm . . .' Durga did not have a clue. 'A dried paan?'

'It is tejpatta.'

Aditya spoke, 'So, will you join me at the lessons? You are a very lucky girl, Durga, do you realize that? Your father is teaching you to become a physician.'

Durga finally had to agree, 'Yes, I will, and I like leaves and fruits too. Baba says I'll be the first lady vaid of Pataliputra.'

Nagasena smiled gently at his daughter's eager face. 'She is my nature girl who wants to wear amaltas earrings.'

At lunchtime, Nagasena and Durga sat before the kitchen as her mother Krishna served them a meal of rice, dal, pumpkin and fish in gravy.

'Aditya will start studying here from tomorrow and he'll have his meals with us whenever he is working with me,' Nagasena said.

'Do monks eat fish and meat?'

'They don't sacrifice animals or birds at the vihara, but he will eat it if we cook here. The Buddha did not want animals to be sacrificed for religious rituals.'

'Good! I hear the monks only eat one meal a day and he is too thin. I'll feed him.' Krishna ate a handful of rice and then asked, 'What did Aditya say about your plan to make your daughter a doctor?'

'He liked the idea very much, but then Buddhists educate everyone, including women, and they don't believe in varna and jati like our priests. Nowhere in our sacred books like the *Charaka Samhita* and the *Sushruta Samhita* does it say that women cannot be doctors.' Nagasena paused. 'Ayurveda means we help people live a long and healthy life. It has nothing to do with what the temple priests say about religion.'

'And if Durga becomes a good doctor,' Krishna replied, nodding, 'patients will come to her, especially women.'

'Exactly!'

Durga decided to join the conversation. 'Amma, I think we should not serve the bhikshu any karela. It is so bitter, he may not like it.'

'Really? Or is it because you don't like it?'

'Umm . . .' She nodded her head. 'That too . . .'

'You will eat karela whenever your amma makes it. Why?'

'It purifies the blood.'

'Very good, my shishya.' Nagasena smiled at his naughty daughter, who dipped her head and said obediently, 'Ji, Guruji,' making her amma and baba laugh.

The next morning, when Aditya arrived, Nagasena asked him, 'Would you object to a small religious ceremony to accept you as my shishya?'

Aditya gave a quick shake of his head. 'Of course not! I would be honoured.'

So, before the sacred fire in the puja room, Nagasena chanted mantras, praying to the gods to give wisdom to his pupil Aditya and then tied a twist of cotton threads around his right wrist and then he took another twist and tied it around Durga's thin, bangled wrist as he intoned, 'And O great Dhanvantri, the physician to the gods, give my daughter Durga patience and kindness so she learns to serve people.'

Aditya and Durga bent and touched their guru's feet as Nagasena blessed them. 'I had requested many vaids to teach me,' Aditya said. 'But they had all refused as I am a follower of the Buddha. I am so grateful you said yes.'

'In return, I want you to make me a promise.'

'Yes, of course!'

'You will never turn away a patient. The poorest, the lowest castes, women and children, they will soon go to the vihara seeking your help and you will do your best to help them. You will not try to make money by only treating the rich.'

'I do not plan to take any fees, Guruji. I am a monk and I do not even touch money. His Majesty Ashoka Vardhan has told us that all the viharas should build free hospitals and libraries for everyone. We do not believe in castes anyway. He has also told us to plant herb gardens and grow food for patients. The work has started already.' Then he looked at a tiny, upturned face and said with a smile, 'Then one day Durga will help me care for the women and children.'

Nagasena placed a loving hand on his daughter's head. 'I am sure she will. You'll just have to plant an amaltas tree at the vihara first.'

When we talk of people living in the past, we think of potters and weavers, water carriers and charioteers and somehow we ignore the mathematicians, astronomers, chemists and doctors. Even in those times, there were people with scientific minds who looked up at the starry skies and wondered about planets and asteroids. Questioning minds studied metals and liquids and there were young people who were bored of memorizing Sanskrit shlokas

and loved numbers and brooded over complicated equations. We had an organized system of medicine called Ayurveda, which so impressed the Greek conqueror Alexander that he took some doctors back to Greece. Our doctors were welcomed at the great city of Baghdad, where the caliphs ruled and many of our books were translated into Arabic and Greek. Our mathematicians were admired around the world and we taught the world an analytical board game called chess.

The problem with our manuscripts, as we now know, is that they were being written on leaves, which crumbled pretty quickly and were often lost forever. Manuscripts survived better in cold climates and English scholars found many ancient manuscripts in the monasteries of Tibet. Two finds in the 19th century CE give

us an idea about ancient mathematics and medicine. In 1881, seventy scattered birch bark leaves were discovered at a place called Bakhshali near Taxila. It is called the Bakhshali manuscript and was written in Prakrit, sometime in the 3rd or 4th century CE. It explains mathematical concepts of fractions, square roots, arithmetic, geometry and equations. It even shows how to work out the square root of a number that is not a perfect square and that means the mathematicians were using the decimal system.

In 1891, a British army man, Hamilton Bower, was camped at a small town called Kuga, which stood on the edge of the Gobi Desert in China. A man offered him a manuscript found at a nearby stupa, which would later be called the Bower Manuscript. The fragments had been part of a book that had belonged to a Buddhist monk named Yashomitra in the 4th or 5th century CE and were buried in a stupa built in his memory. It had three treatises on Ayurveda, the Indian system of medicine, and these are among the oldest we have. Four other treatises were a lot of mumbo jumbo about how to make predictions using dice and incantations against snake bites. Clearly, Yashomitra had some weird interests!

STARRY, STARRY NIGHT

The subsidiaries of the Vedas are called Vedanga. Our ancient knowledge of stars, planets and outer space comes from one such Vedanga. Indians have always liked numbers and complicated calculations, but we also take astrology very seriously, even though it is not scientific at all! So, we studied the stars in astronomy and calculated with mathematics to make predictions in astrology. We wanted to know the auspicious as well as unlucky times of the day; the sacred moments and the dark moments for rituals; which star was lucky and which would bring bad luck. Astrology is called *jyotisha* and our study of astronomy was often aimed at making calculations to set dates for yagyas and other religious rituals. Luckily, our mathematicians also spent time cracking mathematical problems like the value of pi or the circumference of the globe.

We remember some of the astronomers as they wrote books that have survived, the most famous being Aryabhata and Varahamihira in the 5th century CE. Aryabhata was also well known for his knowledge of mathematics and wrote two books—*Aryabhatiya* and *Arya-Siddhanta*. Varahamihira wrote *Panch Siddhanta,* which gathered together the work and ideas on astronomy that had been developed in earlier centuries. However, the problem is that he did not attribute this work to the mathematicians and scientists who did it. Instead, he credited it all to the gods!

Even at a time when travel and communication were difficult, ideas did find their way from China and India to Europe and back along the Silk Road. Arab travellers acted as the messengers, helping Indian scientists and doctors gain awareness of Greek and Roman astronomy. As a matter of fact, Varahamihira mentions theories he called Romaka Siddhanta or Roman Theory. The work on astronomy was not easy as there were no scientific instruments. For example, they had to study the sky without the aid of a telescope day after day to spot the movement of planets and stars and keep careful records.

Indians identified celestial objects in this manner—Surya (sun), Chandra (moon), Budh (Mercury), Shukra (Venus), Brihaspati (Jupiter) and Shani (Saturn). Astrologists believed that these planets influenced the future of people. This first began in Mesopotamia and soon spread across the ancient world. Looking at all the books, websites and newspaper columns, it seems like we still believe that Saturn is evil and Jupiter is good, when they

are just balls of matter circling the sun and have no interest in our puny little lives. And if you think about it logically, no astrologer anywhere on earth predicted the Covid-19 pandemic of 2020! What happened? Didn't Saturn talk to them about this?

CAN YOU TELL ME SOMETHING?

Indians believed that when a demon called Rahu swallowed the sun, we got a solar eclipse and when the demon Ketu swallowed the moon, we got a lunar eclipse. Aryabhata disagreed and explained how the shadow of the earth falling on the moon made the moon disappear from sight and the moon coming between the earth and the sun created a solar eclipse. He also gave the date of equinoxes when the day and night are of equal length and came up with a pretty exact length of a year.

All these calculations were much more accurate than the work of European astronomers. Aryabhata lived in the city of Kusumpura or Pataliputra and he said that the earth rotated on its axis much before European scientists came to the same conclusion. His calculation of the length of a year was 365.2586805 days! Notice he used the decimal system to seven points, without a computer or a calculator.

Varahamihira studied not just the stars but also metals, stones, trees and clouds. His *Brihat Samhita* is an ancient encyclopaedia of science, gathering together all the scientific knowledge of the time.

WE LOVE NUMBERS

Indians have always been good with numbers. The numbers that we use from 0 to 10 are the gift of an unknown mathematician and his imagining the zero is one of the greatest mathematical brainwaves of the world. At that time, the numbering system of the Romans was an unwieldy mix of alphabets like X, M and V, where with larger numbers, it kept getting longer and longer. For example, if you had to write 78, it would be LXXVIII! And even worse, they did not have a zero or any symbol for infinity or a decimal system, but Indian mathematicians used them all.

We called mathematics *ganit shastra* and it grew rapidly during the Gupta period. We had the beginnings of algebra, geometry and trigonometry. Merchants, who had to do calculations for business, immediately began to use the Indian numerical system, which was so easy to use. Arab traders travelling along

the Silk Road soon took it to the Middle East and then Europe. The West originally thought it was an Arab system, but the Arabs always called it Hindusat—Hindu art. Right after this, the Roman numerical system began to die out.

Aryabhata used the decimal system to calculate the value of pi that was more accurate than what Greek mathematicians had calculated. Brahmagupta of the 7th century CE, Mahavira of the 9th century CE and Bhaskara of the 12th century CE did square roots and cube roots, quadratic equations and even calculus, whereas the decimal system was only used in Europe from the 12th century CE. We called the zero *shunya* and it is because of the zero that computer programming became possible in the 19th century CE. So, it is really sad that the name of the mathematical genius who first created a numerical system and then imagined 'nothing' and gave it a symbol has been forgotten. The historian A.L. Basham said, 'The unknown man who devised the new system was from the world's point of view, after the Buddha, the most important son of India.'

LUCKY DAYS AND UNLUCKY HOURS

We have always been believers in astrology and to make predictions, we need accurate calendars. The lunar month follows the waning and waxing of the moon, which means a month is made of two fortnights and a year is made of twelve thirty-day months, which totals up to 360 days. However, the solar year is the time the earth takes to go around the sun and that is 365 days. Our astrological calculations are all done according to the lunar calendar, which is five days short of the solar calendar and so they shift across the solar calendar that is in use in our daily lives. That is why our festivals like Onam and Durga Puja, Diwali and Ganesh Chaturthi have new dates every year.

A lunar day is called a *tithi* and there are thirty in a month. Each month is divided into two fortnights of fifteen days called a *paksha*. During the Shukla Paksha, the moon is waxing ends with the full moon night of *purnima*. The Krishna Paksha is when the moon is waning and ending with the moonless night of *amavasya*. There are twelve lunar months:

Vaisakha	April–May
Jeshtha	May–June
Ashadh	June–July
Shravan	July–August
Bhadra	August–September
Ashvin	September–October
Kartik	October–November
Agrahayan	November–December
Paush	December–January
Magh	January–February
Phalguna	February–March
Chaitra	March–April

Now here is a challenge. Can you name the lunar month to match the solar month of the Roman calendar for your birthday? Or even better, do you know the exact date of your birthday by the lunar calendar? I was born on 10 Ashadh, that is, 24 June.

We also have six seasons, unlike the four common ones of summer, winter, autumn and spring that the rest of the world knows. We have Vasant (spring), Grishma (summer), Varsha (monsoon), Sharad (autumn), Hemanta (winter) and Shishir (the cool season). All this mattered when the astrologer drew up the astrological chart of a person. You'd be surprised to know that astrology did not begin in India. The idea that stars influence our lives began in ancient Mesopotamia and we took the idea of astrological symbols

from the Greek and called them *rashi*. We just translated the names and symbols into Sanskrit. So Leo became Simha rashi or the lion; Libra, Tula rashi or weighing scales, and Capricorn, Makara rashi or crocodile; the symbols remained the same like the fish for Mina rashi or Pisces; the crab for Karkata rashi or Cancer.

WHAT IS THE UNIVERSE MADE OF?

The dictionary states that physics is the branch of science concerned with the nature and properties of matter and energy, which really just means everything that makes up our world has to do with physics. Our ancient scholars or rishis had one thing in common—they had very curious minds and not all of them were thinking holy, spiritual thoughts. They loved to ask questions. And the very basic question of what makes up our physical world was naturally one of them. How do clouds travel across the sky? How do rivers flow? What is the smallest particle to make up our world? Their curious minds brooded over such questions even though they had no laboratories to help them.

By the time of Gautama Buddha, 2500 years ago, our rishis had been asking and speculating about many things around us. They listed the elements that make up the universe as five—earth, air, fire, water and ether. The last element is a bit hard to understand because we had to wonder how it was different from air. According to them, the smallest object to occupy space, so small we could not see it, was called *anu*, which is similar to the atom or maybe the molecule. They said this even though there were no microscopes. The atom is the smallest particle of a chemical element and a molecule is a group of atoms bonded together. Our scientifically minded rishis were working with their vivid imagination to find an explanation for the structure of the world.

So, if you thought rishis were these ancient guys with long white beards who did *yagyas* and gave lectures about karma and dharma, you are mistaken. They were scholars of many subjects and were asking questions around science and that led to developments in fields like metallurgy and chemistry. Think of the Iron Pillar in the Qutub Complex in Delhi. It is our metallurgists who created an iron that has stood in the sun and rain for centuries and not rusted. Our chemists were using their knowledge of the elements, plants and metals to mix and create medicines and were learning what chemicals could cure disease through experiments. So, we had many kinds of scientists—physicists, chemists and metallurgists and many of them, like the mathematicians, were far ahead of the Europeans.

HOW ARE YOU FEELING TODAY?

Just as we have doctors' clinics and hospitals in our localities, the ancient physicians were called vaids and they practised a system of medicine called Ayurveda. Over two thousand years later, Ayurveda is still practised in India as an alternate system of healing. *Ayu* means 'age' and Ayurveda means the science for a long and healthy life through a system of balanced living. There were three experts called the Great Triad who gathered our knowledge of medicine into books—Charaka, who wrote the *Charaka Samhita* in the 2nd century CE, Sushruta's *Sushruta Samhita* dated to around 600 CE and Vagbhata, who wrote *Ashtanga Hridayam* around the 7th century CE. Initially, this knowledge was limited to Brahmins, but the Buddhist monks, who did not believe in the caste system, were happy to share their knowledge with the world. They did great service by writing down all the medical information in their monasteries and spreading the practice of Ayurveda.

Emperor Ashoka built free hospitals and planted herb gardens for making medicines. This system so impressed the Greek conqueror Alexander that he took some vaids back to Greece with him. Later, a mix of Ayurveda, Greek and Arab medicine came back to India with the Muslims and came to be known as the Unani system, which is still in practice today. We also had veterinary sciences and the book *Hastyayurveda*, written by Palakapya, was for the treatment of elephants.

The *Charaka Samhita* is a sort of a big encyclopaedia of medicine with 120 chapters divided into eight sections. It covers topics like disease, how to examine a patient and diagnose their illness and their treatment with medicines and food. The human body and the functions of the organs are described and Charaka, who clearly did not like the brain, believed that our intelligence came from the heart. In fact, he said nothing about the functions of the brain.

The *Sushruta Samhita* has instructions on surgery. It has six sections called *sutras* and gives details of a doctor's training; how to make medicines; the diet recommended for different ailments; symptoms of various diseases, diagnosis and surgery. Of course, the knowledge of the human anatomy was limited as the vaids did not want to touch corpses due to their caste and hence did not perform any anatomical studies. Our surgeons were famous world over for their skills and doctors travelled to India to study from them.

Indian surgeons were the first to perform a form of cataract surgery in the world and could also remove stones in the bladder. Doctors often had to treat soldiers who were wounded in battle and they knew how to suture the injuries and how torn earlobes were repaired.

Indian surgeons developed the earliest form of plastic surgery too—as a need to reconstruct noses as cutting them off was a common punishment for prisoners of war. They took a flap of skin from the forehead and created a new nose. They also knew how to birth babies surgically, a method that's now termed a 'caesarean delivery'. English surgeons of the East India Company were learning surgical techniques from Indian surgeons as late as 18th century CE.

Ayurveda believes that three semi-liquid substances called *vata*, *pitta* and *kapha* circulate in our body and for good health, they must be kept in balance. They are translated a bit vaguely as 'wind', 'bile' and 'phlegm' and they are the dosha or the biological process and *dhatu*, that is, the body tissue. Vaids would examine a patient carefully and judge their temperament before prescribing any medicine. Patients would be divided into categories: the *sattvik* or calm person, the *rajasik* or excitable person and the *tamasik* or courageous person. The treatment was according to the temperament of the patient. Now what would a vaid do if the patient was both a calm and a brave person?

In Ayurveda, a balanced diet is crucial for health. A balanced meal had to be a combination of the six tastes or rasas—sweet, sour, salty, bitter, pungent and astringent like ginger. Medicines, called *aushadhi*, were prescribed during an illness and regular exercise was recommended. So right from those ancient times, doctors were talking of a healthy lifestyle, saying do not overeat, go for walks and take the right medicines. That hasn't changed, has it?

Vaids saw patients in their own homes but also made house calls when needed. They did not have a stethoscope or a blood pressure machine but they checked the pulse and made a very careful examination of the patients while asking questions to come to a diagnosis. They would prescribe a diet and make the medicine for each patient using herbs and minerals. Sushruta mentions 700 medicinal herbs. The Chinese traveller Hsuan Tsang mentions houses dispensing food and medicine to the poor and Charaka gives detailed instructions on how to equip and run a hospital.

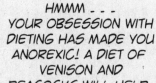

As he wrote, the ideal hospital would have a clean airy building in a quiet locality with clean water supply. Toilets, bathing areas and a kitchen had to be built and kept clean. Then a staff of nurses, cooks, bathing attendants, masseurs and herb grinders had to be employed. He even said that the staff had to be kind and courteous. One of his ideas that we could introduce in our hospitals is soothing music and a storyteller.

Four

SINGERS, DRUMMERS AND FLUTE PLAYERS

Jaiwant looked around with wide, shining eyes and thought, *I am in jannat! This has to be paradise on earth!*

Nine-year-old Jaiwant and his father, the famous painter Daswant, were sitting at Anup Talao, in Emperor Akbar's magnificent city of Fatehpur Sikri. Here the royal musicians sang to their king and artists from the royal painter's atelier called the Tasvir Khana sketched the gorgeous scene. Later they would create a miniature painting of the concert for the king and many would be included in the books in the royal library. This evening, it was Daswant's turn to sketch the scene and he sat under a lamp with a small bundle of handmade paper and a bunch of charcoal sticks.

'Baba, who is singing today?' Jaiwant tilted his head up to look up at his father's face. 'Is it Baz Bahadur?'

'No, it is Mian Tansen.'

'Ohhh…' Jaiwant breathed happily. 'The great Tansen himself! And you will paint him. *Kya baat!*'

'Yes. Don't forget, Jaiwant, you can talk now.' Daswant frowned at his son. 'But once the badshah arrives, you will stay very quiet.'

'Ji, Bauji.'

'Children are not allowed at a royal concert. I had to take special permission to bring you here.'

'Ji, Bauji …' Jaiwant knew he talked too much, everyone said so. *I am not stupid*, he thought rebelliously, *I know when to keep quiet!*

'The badshah is here!' someone whispered and Jaiwant turned eagerly to look.

Anup Talao was a small lotus pool in the middle of a big red sandstone courtyard. On one side was the palace called Khwabgah, the palace of dreams, and Emperor Akbar was walking out of it, surrounded by his friends. A short, stocky figure, he was busy chatting with his best friends—the historian Abul Fazl and the poet Raja Birbal, who said something that made the king throw back his head and laugh aloud.

All around the pool, carpets had been laid and covered with white sheets and here the men of the royal family and the noblemen sat leaning against bolsters. There was a square stone seat in the centre of the pool, where Tansen would sit and sing. The pillars of the palaces had garlands of flowers wrapped around them and bowls of rose petals sat by the walls, filling the air with their fragrance. As Jaiwant watched, maids came out carrying small oil lamps on brass thalis and floated the lamps on the water of the pool. The starry sky was now reflected in the water. Tall metal lamps stood in the corners, creating a halo of golden light and the air smelled of flowers and incense.

Jaiwant had seen Akbar before because the king often dropped in at the Tasvir Khana to look at the work of the artists. Whom he wished he could see were the queens and princesses of the Mughal family—the queen mother Hamida Banu Begum, Akbar's aunt Gulbadan Begum, his senior-ranking queen Salima Sultan Begum and the Rajput queen Mariam-uz-Zamani. He was sure they had all come for the concert but sat hidden behind *chik* curtains at one end of the courtyard near the harem. He could see their shadows moving behind the curtain and hear the chink of their bangles.

There was a stir in the audience as Tansen entered, followed by two students, who carried tanpuras, and a pakhawaj player carrying his drum. They walked along the narrow walkway to the seat in the centre of the pool. Tansen wore a cream silk achkan that was embroidered in gold, a pearl necklace and pearl earrings. Jaiwant turned to see his father busy sketching the singer's face.

Mian Tansen began to sing a *dhrupad* that someone behind them whispered was set in Raga Darbari Kanhra, the new raga he had composed in praise of the king. In the beginning, Jaiwant listened carefully, but after a while he began to get a bit bored. The audience was going 'Wah! Wah!' in praise, the king was shaking his head to the beat of the pakhawaj, but Jaiwant realized he did not really understand the music at all!

He thought, *I like the qawwali they sing at the tomb of the Sufi saint Sheikh Salim Chishti and the bhajans they sing at the temples, but what is this music without any words?* Instead, he sat and watched his father draw and was a bit relieved when the concert drew to an end. Mian Tansen bowed before his king and was given a big bag of gold mohur coins and another bag was sent by the women of the harem.

Everyone was saying that it was an outstanding performance but Jaiwant was half asleep. *I'd rather be a painter than a singer,* he thought a bit woozily. *I could fall asleep while singing and then the badshah would get angry.*

It was a long walk from Anup Talao to their home, which was a small, whitewashed house right behind the Tasvir Khana. Jaiwant wandered along by his father's side, yawning away.

Noticing his son's drooping eyelids, Daswant asked with a laugh, 'The music put you to sleep, kya?'

'It did. One concert is enough for me, thank you. I'll never bother you to take me to Anup Talao again.'

'I told you that you would not like it and a concert goes on for hours, but when do you listen to me?'

'I still want to watch the dancers,' He muttered stubbornly.

'I'll think about it. To watch the dancers, I'll have to go to the Diwan-i-Aam where the badshah holds his public audience. I may not be sent there for months.'

'*Theek hai.* I'll wait.'

They walked along silently through the dark streets that were lit by the fire of oil torches. It was a moonlit night and the silver light made it easier to walk under the starry sky. Daswant was softly humming the last song that Tansen had sung.

'Bauji . . .' Jaiwant began.

'You have a question . . .' his father sighed.

'You know I always do.' Jaiwant smiled. 'Now tell me . . . Is Mian Tansen a Hindu or a Muslim?'

'He is a singer,' his father said shortly.

'Yes, I know *that*!' Jaiwant persisted. 'When I told my friend Badlu I was going to the concert, he told me that Tansen's wife is called Husseini Begum, his sons are named Bilas Khan and Tanras Khan, but his daughter is called Saraswati. Now I know that Saraswati is a goddess that we worship as Hindus. And today Mian Tansen sang a thumri in Raga Bhairava, which is in praise of Lord Shiva, and Raga Durga, which is a song for the warrior goddess! Does that mean he worships our gods and goddesses and he also prays to Allah?'

'What am I?' his father asked.

'You are a painter.'

'Does it matter that I am a lower-caste son of a *kahar* and my father was a poor palki bearer?'

'Of course not! When you were a boy, the badshah saw you paint and brought you to the Tasvir Khana,' Jaiwant replied with a proud sniff. 'You are the best painter in the Tasvir Khana.'

'In the same way, he brought Mian Tansen to Fatehpur Sikri because he is the greatest singer in the kingdom. His religion does not matter.'

'I agree, Bauji,' Jaiwant said stubbornly, 'but you did not answer my question—is he a Muslim or a Hindu?'

'He is both. He is a Hindu who married a Muslim lady and named his daughter after the goddess of knowledge and music.'

'So when he sings, which god is he praying to?'

'He prays and sings to the Supreme Being. Say any name you like—Allah, Shiva, Saraswati, God is one and the same.'

Jaiwant frowned. 'So many people to pray to! That sounds complicated. I think I'll just pray to Hanumanji. I like him.'

'Do that.' There was laughter is his father's voice. 'And what will you say to Hanumanji?'

'I'll say, "Please, Hanumanji, make me a great painter like my bauji."'

'I am a Hindu, my teacher at the Tasvir Khana, Ustad Abdus Samad, is a Muslim. He taught me how to draw and use the many colours on the palette. All those colours that I use, what religion are they?'

'They are just colours.'

Daswant ruffled his son's hair. 'Exactly! Just as a song is just music.'

Jaiwant yawned in reply.

~~~~~~

Can you imagine the amazing experience of listening to Mian Tansen sing at the Anup Talao in Fatehpur Sikri? His deep baritone soaring up to the starry sky and touching our hearts, as music has the power to touch us in ways that we cannot imagine. The Mughal historian Abul Fazl, in his book *Ain-i-Akbari*, gives a long list of singers who performed in the court of Emperor Akbar. Among them were Mian Tansen and Baz Bahadur, who was the former king of Malwa. Baz Bahudur was not too interested in running a kingdom and much preferred to sing.

Anup Talao still stands, though Akbar's city—Fatehpur Sikri—lies empty except for visiting tourists and wandering ghosts. If you stand beside Anup Talao as the sun is going down and listen carefully, you can hear the ghostly echo of the voice of a singer who worshipped all the gods of every religion through his celestial music. We have not forgotten Mian Tansen after five centuries and we have not forgotten Daswant either. In Akbar's atelier of miniature painters, a set of paintings, called Ragmala, were done to capture the moods of various ragas. Daswant may have done one of Raga Bhairavi, inspired by the singing of Mian Tansen.

WE ALL SING

Music is a part of our lives and we all sing, even if it may not always be in tune! We sing bhajans while doing puja at the temple, we listen to the Shabad Kirtan at gurdwaras, sing hymns in church and sway to qawwalis in dargahs. There are religious songs like the *abhangs* in Marathi that were composed by poets like Namdev, Tukaram and Eknath. Odissi dancers perform to the songs of Jaideva in Oriya and there is the poetry of Mirabai and Kabir and Bhakti poets like Andal and Sundarar, whose poetry is sung in the temples of the south, and the *shabads* of Guru Nanak that are sung every day in Sikh gurdwaras.

There are songs sung during weddings, festivals and religious rituals. Music is everywhere, on television, on the radio and on our mobile phones.

Accompanying singers are the players of musical instruments that are categorized in the Natya Shastra by Bharata, the oldest book on the performing arts, probably written in the 5th century CE. There are *tat vadya* or stringed instruments like the sitar and veena; *sushira vadya* or wind instruments like the flute and shehnai; *avanaddha vadya* or percussion instruments like the various kinds of drums; and *ghana vadya* or solid instruments like earthen pots and bells.

In India, we have two styles of classical music called Hindustani and Carnatic. Mian Tansen and Pandit Bhimsen Joshi sang in the Hindustani style of North India, whereas Thyagaraja and M.S. Subbulakshmi sang in the Carnatic traditions of

South India. Then there are the popular and lighter forms of music like the bhajans, kirtans, hymns and qawwalis. There are songs like thumri, *dadra*, *chaiti*, *lavani* and *baul*, which are a mix of classical and folk tunes. Urdu poetry is sung in a ghazal. Rabindra Sangeet, based on the poetry of Rabindranath Tagore, and Nazrul Geeti, based on the poetry of Kazi Nazrul Islam, are much loved styles of Bengal. We have songs sung on stage and mouthed by actors in films. Today, with khayal and *kritis*, thumris and *bhatiyali*, we also have rock and rap, reggae and beat and the music just goes on . . .

JUST SEVEN NOTES

It all began with priests chanting the poetry of the Rig Veda—a prayer to their gods as they sat before the altar of the yagya fire. The poetry in the Vedas was composed in praise of the gods of the ancient Aryans and as prayers. So even today, when priests sway and chant mantras and recite shlokas, they are praying to Agni, the god of fire, or Indra, the god of thunder and lightning. For centuries, this poetry was memorized and not written down and one way to memorize was by singing the verses. For over three thousand years, the poetry has remained pretty much intact though, at times, we no longer know the meaning of the ancient Sanskrit words!

All our music is based on the seven notes of the sargam: sa-re-ga-ma-pa-dha-ni. In the North, they are referred to as *sajda*, *rishabha*, *gandhara*, *madhyama*, *panchama*, *dharvata* and *nishada*. With it, there are half notes that make the music both simple and complex at the same time. A classical music concert can be about knowing the intricacies of the notes of a raga and the rhythms of the tala, but it can also be about just listening and enjoying the beauty of the song. You really don't have to be an expert on ragas or understand the intricacy of the beats of the drums. Good music always speaks to us.

The Natya Shastra talks about music, dance and theatre and proves that our music had a pretty precise set of rules. A classical music performance is primarily a combination of a raga, a melody and a tala—the rhythm in which it is to be sung. So we need a poet for the words and a musician to compose the tune for a concert. Very often, our greatest singers have also been poets. Indian classical music has no tradition of an orchestra and usually musicians perform alone. Western classical music lacks the tala system and operates on a different system. The beat or tala is very important in Indian classical music as we like to tap our hands and feet and shake our heads as we listen to music.

RAGA, TALA, SWARA

All music is a combination of three elements—raga, tala and *swara*. The word raga is hard to translate into English. It means mood or colour but also passion. A raga, with its medley of musical notes, sets the mood and feelings of a song, whether it is happy or sad, solemn or joyous. The tala is the rhythm of a performance and this beat is played by percussion instruments like the tabla or the mridangam. Swara means sound and it is called swara when the notes are sung by a human voice. So a vocal musical performance has to be a combination of poetry and music, the rhythm and the human voice expressing it.

Like Mian Tansen, a singer was a poet and a poet was often also a singer. In Hindustani music, the raga is set to a small poem called bandish, which is composed with a fixed number and combination of five or more notes of the sargam. The singer is free to mix them in many combinations,

THAT'S THE EFFECT
OF SOME HAPPY RAGA
WHICH FILLS YOU
WITH JOY I GUESS.

I CAN SEE THAT.

creating newer tunes. This means that a singer can create a new melody right there on stage before an audience, so no two performances are the same. This is very different from Western classical music, in which the piece is written down on paper and performed exactly the same way every time. In the khayal style of singing, the singer begins with wordless singing, called alap, and moves into different beats in the *bol*, when the words are sung. Then the singing gets faster in the *gamaka* and ends with a combination of words and tune, in the section called the *antara*. They improvise and sing the tune differently every time.

In Carnatic music, the lyrics of the raga are composed in a poem called kriti and they are much longer than the bandish. A tune is composed for each kriti with melody and rhythm and the singer sticks to that tune. So there is less improvisation during a performance of the kriti compared to Hindustani music, in which the notes are like paint that a singer mixes to create a new painting every time and the words of the bandish are really just a part of the mood. Hindustani music evolved over centuries as it was put into systems by singers of many schools of music.

The Natya Shastra mentions thirty ragas and twenty-two talas, but through the centuries, singers have created many new ragas. The text mentions six basic ragas—all sung at different times of the day: Bhairava at dawn; Megha in the morning; Deepak and Sri in the afternoon; and Kaushiki and Hindola at night. Ragas are also connected to seasons: Raga Megh Malhar is sung during the rains and Raga Basant in spring, especially during the festival of Holi. Each raga is created around emotions. Bhairava is a hymn in praise of Lord Shiva and the notes express awe and fear in a powerful, soaring melody. Kaushiki has softer notes and captures the feelings of joy and laughter. The melody and bandish speak of love in Hindola, Deepak and Sri. The quiet and calm notes of Megha express peace and serenity.

PALLAVI WHO?

Carnatic music is different from Hindustani music in many ways. The most important of these is that Hindustani music had rajas and nawabs as patrons and their themes were of the courtly world. In the south, musicians were attached to temples and they sang of their devotion to the deities. Many saint-singers composed kritis that are sung in a system called *ragam-tanam-pallavi*. The kriti is always based on a raga and is first sung without words in the *alapana*, which has no clear beat, then with a beat in the section called tanam. Finally, in pallavi, there is a blend of poetry and melody that is set to a beat.

These traditions were organized by Purandara Dasa in the 15th century CE and taught by gurus to their students. The three greatest composers of this music, who created a wonderful collection of kritis in the 18th and 19th century CE,

were Shyama Shastri (1762–1827), Thyagaraja (1767–1847) and Muthuswami Dikshitar (1775–1835). Surprisingly, all three musicians were born in the town of Thiruvarur in the Thanjavur district of Tamil Nadu. They composed songs in Sanskrit, Tamil and Telugu and they are still sung today. Thyagaraja is said to have composed over a thousand kritis and around 700 still survive. Just as we can imagine Mian Tansen performing at Fatehpur Sikri, we can imagine these great composers singing before the deities at great temples like Brihadishwara in Thanjavur.

OUR GREAT MIANJI!

The story of Mian Tansen is quite an adventurous tale. He was the son of a village temple priest and he was named Ramtanu Pandey. One day, the great singer Swami Haridas of Vrindavan heard him sing and took him on as a student. Later, Ramtanu went to Gwalior to learn music from the Sufi teacher Muhammad Ghaus and he married Ghaus's daughter Husseini.

Ramtanu became famous as the court singer of Raja Ramchandra Dev, the king of Rewa and it was this king who gave him the title of Tansen. Emperor Akbar, who liked to have the finest creative talents in his court, then requested that Ramchandra Dev send Tansen to his court at Fatehpur Sikri and who could refuse the emperor? So Tansen arrived at Fatehpur Sikri, where he often sang at Anup Talao. It is said that Akbar gifted him with Rs 2 lakh for his first concert and he affectionately called him 'Mian'.

A Hindustani school of music is called a gharana and Tansen founded the Agra gharana where his sons Bilas Khan and Tanras Khan and daughter Saraswati were all singers. So it is possible that Saraswati sang for the women in the Mughal harem. They all taught music and created new ragas like their father, many of which have survived till today. Tansen sang in the style called dhrupad, which is mostly wordless, purely music and requires great skill at voice control. Tansen composed ragas like Mian ki Malhar, Mian ki Todi and Darbari Kanhra. Legend has it that he could make it rain by singing Raga Malhar and lamps would light up spontaneously when he sang Raga Deepak. The khayal style that is popular nowadays would be developed later in Delhi in the 19th century CE by a singer called Niamat Khan, who wrote poems under the pen name of Sadarang.

In Fatehpur Sikri, there is a small round building with a veranda that tourist guides say was where Tansen lived. Imagine how lucky you would be if you lived close by and woke up every morning to an alap sung by the greatest singer in the kingdom! Tansen's grave is in Gwalior, next to the mausoleum of his Sufi teacher Muhammad Ghaus. There is a tamarind tree next to his grave and it is said that chewing its sour leaves makes your voice more tuneful. In Hindi, the word for ears is *kaan* and there is an old joke that people who can't sing but are very good listeners are called Kansen!

WHO IS SINGING TONIGHT?

All through history, there was nothing like a live musical performance to understand classical music. The excited audience gathered before the stage and the performance could be anywhere—in an auditorium, inside a tent, under the stars, on a beach by the sea or on a hillside. First the musicians who accompany the singer would enter to loud applause. In a Hindustani concert there would be the percussionist—a tabla player and at times, a player with the narrow single drum called the pakhawaj. A musician playing the stringed sarangi sat opposite and two people sat behind the singer, playing the tanpura, adding a soft droning background sound.

Today, at Hindustani classical concerts, the main attraction is the khayal, which has replaced the dhrupad that was sung by Tansen. This style uses a bandish and various ways of singing the raga. First there is the alap, then the bol, the fast-paced *gamaka*, the *khatka*, *sthayi* and antara. Over the centuries, Sanskrit was replaced by Hindi and its dialects like Bhojpuri and Awadhi. As rulers, like the Mughals, came from other countries like Persia, Hindustani music was also influenced by Persian styles and moved away from dhrupad, which resembled the Sanskrit Vedic chants of prayers. There are more accompanists in a Carnatic music concert. Instead of the tabla, we have a drum called mridangam, a flute and a violin instead of the sarangi. Then there is the ghatam, which is really an earthen pot and a tambourine-like instrument called kanjira. Only the tanpuras are the same.

PRACTICE . . . PRACTICE . . .

Our Hindustani classical music is not taught in a classroom, but in schools of music called gharanas. You cannot become a classical musician without a teacher and it is a teacher, guru or ustad who trains and hones the talent of a student. This is not just for singing but also for playing musical instruments. This is the 'guru-shishya *parampara*' or the teacher-student tradition of musical training.

The family members of a guru are trained, of course, but even other talented young people are accepted as students—the *shagird* or shishya. What follows are years of training at practice sessions called *riyaz* or sadhana. Even famous and experienced musicians never stop doing riyaz, which is essential to keep your musical talent at its finest state. Tansen had his gurus Swami Haridas and Muhammad Ghaus.

In recent times, there was Ustad Allauddin Khan, who began the Maihar gharana and was the ustad to many famous musicians like his son Ali Akbar, who played the sarod; his daughter Annapurna, who played the *surbahar* and Ravi Shankar, the sitar player who became famous across the world when he became the guru of the Beatles member George Harrison. Ravi Shankar played a big role in popularizing Indian classical music in the West, even performing with the famous violinist Yehudi Menuhin.

FROM GODS TO GURUS

For us, music really begins with the gods. Saraswati is the goddess of not just knowledge but also music. She is the creator of the Vedas and she sits on a lotus, clad in white, with her pet swan perched at her feet. She plays the veena, which is the earliest string instrument and came before the sitar and the sarod. It is said that Ravana, the king of Lanka, was a great musician who created the rudra veena and composed the Raga Rudra, dedicated to Shiva. The sage Rishi Narada, who is often a source of gossip in our mythological stories, is always shown carrying a veena. Does that mean he sang out all the latest news to the gods? And the musicians who entertained our deities in heaven were called *gandharvas*.

All through history, kings and nobility patronized musicians. Members of a gharana would perform at the royal court like the Jaipur gharana and the Gwalior gharana. All the Mughal kings except Aurangzeb encouraged musicians, but he banned music and dance in court. As a response, all the dancers and musicians took out a funeral procession through the streets of Delhi, weeping and wailing at the death of their art. Sadly, Aurangzeb was unmoved. A later Mughal king, Muhammad Shah, was called *rangila* or 'colourful' as he patronized many musicians and among them was Niamat Khan, who created the musical style called khayal.

Rulers like Ibrahim Adil Shah of Bijapur, Karnataka; Baz Bahadur of Malwa, Madhya Pradesh; Wajid Ali Shah of Awadh, Uttar Pradesh; and Swathi Thirunal of Travancore, Kerala, were kings who were talented poets and singers. Wajid Ali Shah composed songs under the pen name of Akhtar Piya and would sing in praise of Lord Krishna. The extraordinary Swathi Thirunal composed over four hundred songs set to both

Carnatic and Hindustani styles. At the same time, he was an able ruler who knew nine Indian languages. Now, when you are so talented, you deserve a long name to match and his full name was Sree Padmanabhadasa Sree Swathi Thirunal Rama Varma Kulashekhara Perumal.

Over the centuries, we have had many legendary singers like Baiju Bawra and Baz Bahadur who sang at the same time as Tansen. What is unique about our musicians is that music was their religion and they sang with equal devotion for all deities. The last wish of the Sufi saint Sheikh Salim Chishti was that Tansen should sing for him and chances are, he would have sung a dhrupad prayer to a Hindu god. In the 17th century CE, Ibrahim Adil Shah wrote a book called *Kitab-i-Nauras* and composed songs to both Muslim saints and Hindu gods. He sang in the Carnatic style and was an ardent devotee of the goddess Saraswati and proudly bore the Hindu title 'Jagad Guru'. Just like in our time, Pandit Jasraj set a song to Raga Bhairavi and sang 'Mero Allah Meherbaan'.

As they would all have said, music has no caste or religion, it is just music and everyone is welcome in their magnificent world of a passion called raga.

Five

DANCERS, ACTORS AND PLAYWRIGHTS

Revati picked up the broom from the courtyard and headed back to the house, yawning. She had overslept again and had to dust and mop the practice room before her mistress Padmalaya came downstairs from her bedroom. The floor had to be smooth, shining and dry when she began her morning dance rehearsal. Revati just wished that Padmalaya would not get up so early. The sun had barely come up, the cocks had just started crowing and most of the nearby homes were still dark and quiet. It was only Padmalaya who refused to sleep in and Revati did not understand why!

'Just my bad luck,' Revati grumbled to herself as she wielded the broom with an irritated flick of her wrist. 'Just because you are a famous dancer of Vijayanagar, it doesn't mean you make your maid, your poor little maid, get up at dawn every day!' She dumped the mopping cloth into the bucket of water. 'Don't maids have the right to sleep a little when they work so hard all day?'

Soon the floor had been wiped and was now wet and gleaming. When Padmalaya danced, if she felt even a small sliver of grit under her feet, she would stop and yell, 'Revati! I see dirt!' and poor Revati would have to run in with a broom to clean the floor once again. That is why she sat and watched the floor dry because today's practice was very important.

Revati was twelve years old and she had been working at Padmalaya's home for a month now. Her father was a cook in a food shop in the bazaar of the Virupaksha Temple. One day, Padmalaya's gardener came to eat at the food shop and said the dancer was looking for a maid. She wanted a young girl who would clean the rehearsal room, help her with her clothes, comb

her hair, weave garlands, polish her jewellery, grind sandalwood for her puja and make kohl . . . It was a long list of jobs. Revati's father had come home that evening and announced that he had found Revati a job! The list of chores kept Revati busy all day. She quite liked the work except for having to get up so early. The salary, her amma said, was very good and the food was wonderful. She thought of the previous night's dinner, which was fish in coconut sauce and tamarind rice.

Her eyelids began to droop as she sat curled up in the corner of the room.

'Revati!' The shrill call made her sit up, her heart thudding. 'Where are you?'

She scrambled up and ran up the stairs to Padmalaya's bedroom. She gathered up a fresh set of clothes, oil and soap and followed her to the pond, where the dancer had a long bath. By the time they came back to the room Revati had just cleaned, Padmalaya's mother, Parvati Amma, was waiting for them. She helped Revati dry and comb Padmalaya's long hair, put on a sari and wear gold jewellery—a necklace, bangles and earrings.

'Tonight, you will wear much more!' Parvati Amma smiled at her daughter. 'You will look like a queen.'

Padmalaya gave a shake of her head. 'I'm so nervous, Amma! It is the king. If he does not like my performance, they will send me back to the temple.'

'They will like it.' Parvati Amma tried to calm her daughter. 'I know they will.'

Before the musicians arrived, Revati rushed to the kitchen for her breakfast because she wanted to watch her mistress dance. She sat down on the floor with a banana leaf. Then, as the cook

Madhava served her idlis and coconut chutney, he asked, 'The floor is shining clean, I hope?'

'Of course it is.' Revati bit into an idli and nodded impatiently. He asked the question every day. Then she frowned. 'Uncle, was Padmalaya always like this?'

'Like what?' He was busy chopping spinach.

'She is always angry with me, she is never happy with my work.'

'She is young and this is her first performance before the king.'

'But she dances so well!'

Madhava said that Parvati Amma and Padmalaya were temple dancers who danced before the god. There were other dancers too and only the best were asked to perform when King Krishnadevaraya came to Virupaksha Temple. This was the first time that Padmalaya had been chosen to dance before His Majesty.

'If the royal family likes her performance, she will become a senior dancer like her mother. Then she will be invited to dance at the palace and come back with bags of gold coins and even jewellery if the queens are pleased by the show.'

'Ah!' Revati now understood. She licked the last of the chutney and said, 'You dance well, you become super rich!'

'You get a big house, wear silks and jewels, have many servants and have the biggest palanquin!'

'And eat fish every day . . .'

Madhava laughed. 'You only think of food, you greedy girl.'

'My appa is also a cook, remember?'

All morning, Padmalaya rehearsed and Revati sat in a corner and watched, entranced by her dancing. *She moves like a swan*, Revati thought admiringly as the mridangam kept the beat and the singer sang the padam and the *nattuvanar* kept the beat by tapping on a piece of wood. Padmalaya's eyes moved, her lips smiled, her fingers told a story through the mudras as the bells of her anklet jangled. Then, moving like a swift bird, she danced across the room with dazzling footwork. It took Revati's breath away.

In the evening, with Revati helping, Parvati Amma dressed her daughter. Padmalaya's long hair was braided with golden thread and flowers. Her large eyes were lined with kohl to make them look even larger and her lips were reddened with paan juice.

Then she drew an intricate tilak on her daughter's forehead between the eyebrows. Revati painted Padmalaya's feet with red lac and drew a pattern on her palms.

'Get the jewellery box, Revati,' said Parvati Amma, once Padmalaya had put on the pleated sari.

Two small brooches shaped like the sun and the moon were put on her hair and a gold thread with a pendant called *netti chutti* placed in the parting of her hair. Her nose ring was set with pearls and her small earrings, the *thodus*, gleamed beside her cheeks. The crocodile-shaped *vankhi* armlets snaked up her elbows. Around her neck she wore the *mangamalai* with mango-shaped pendants and a long chain. Her gold *mekhala* belt went across her hips. Revati bent and tied her heavy belled anklets.

Revati looked up at Padmalaya, her eyes shining. 'You really do look like a goddess, Akka.'

Padmalaya looked down at the admiring young face and her eyed softened. 'Do you think I'll dance well tonight, Revati?'

'Yes, you will,' said Revati firmly. 'You will dance like a butterfly and the king will fall in love with you.'

Parvati Amma laughed.

As the sun began to fade, tall metal lamps were lit all around the courtyard of the temple. The spectators sat all around, but the space before the temple sanctum was kept empty because Padmalaya would dance before the god, Lord Shiva. King Krishnadevaraya and his two queens sat on a high seat, leaning against bolsters and everyone was clad in shimmering silks and glittering jewellery.

Padmalaya entered to the roll of the mridangam and Revati took a deep breath. She first danced slowly, charming the audience with her sinuous movements and then in the *varnam*, she began to tell a story through her eyes and lips and the movement of her fingers. The voice of the nattuvanar rose as he recited the complex beat that she danced the speedy scintillating *tillana* to, whirling and spinning, stamping her feet and curving her arms in a dazzling presentation of pure dance.

When Padmalaya brought her performance to an end and bowed, the audience was silent for a second and then exploded in applause. She bowed at the king's feet and Krishnadevaraya touched her head in blessing and gave her a bag of coins. The queens each placed one gold and one pearl necklace around her neck too. Revati looked up at Parvati Amma's shining face and smiled.

~~~~~~

This dance performance during the reign of King Krishnadevaraya of Vijayanagar would have taken place in the 16th century CE. The dance would have been Bharatanatyam, one of the classical dances of India, and the dancer would have danced before the shrine of Lord Shiva, who was also called Nataraja, the lord of dance.

THE GOD WHO DANCES

Indian classical dance begins with mythology as it is said that many gods and goddesses enjoy dancing. The plump and happy Ganesha dances holding his favourite sweets, modaks, while the goddess Kali dances in forests; she once even challenged Shiva to a dance contest. Krishna often dances the Raas with the *gopis*

THIS IS CALLED THE MODAK DANCE.

of Vrindavan. The god who is the best dancer of all is Shiva as Nataraja and his dance is called the *tandava*. Shiva dances when he is happy, but also when he is angry. In his happy mood, he dances in heaven, which we call Swarga, before a gathering of gods and goddesses. Saraswati plays the veena, Indra blows on a flute, Brahma plays the cymbals and Lakshmi sings as Vishnu keeps the beat on the drums. It is a truly celestial performance.

In Hindu mythology, Brahma is the creator of the universe, Vishnu is the caretaker and then as the yuga or cycle comes to an end, Shiva destroys it all so that creation can begin again.

He does so by dancing the tandava in anger and everything below his feet, all the evil in the world that set off his fury, ends. As fires begin to burn everything down, the universe turns to dust and ashes at his madly dancing feet. The image of Shiva as Nataraja that we are all familiar with is of him dancing the tandava. He stands with his left foot raised and under his right foot lies a dwarf called Apasmara, the demon of ignorance. Nataraja is surrounded by a circle of flames. He has four arms, one right hand holds a small drum called *damaru* and the other is raised in a gesture of kindness called *nirbhaya*. One left hand holds a ball of fire and the other points down to Apasmara.

Shiva wears a lot of jewellery though some are rather unusual. As he moves quickly, his long hair whirls around his face like a halo and in his hair, he wears the moon and the river goddess Ganga, with a cobra coiled around his neck like a necklace. Like dancers of today, he wears a short dhoti, his chest is bare, he

wears bangles, a jewelled belt and anklets with bells. He looks so majestic you forget he is destroying the world.

This image shows how amazingly talented the craftspeople who composed this visual were. They understood the meaning of the tandava and created this extraordinary image that captures perfectly the portrayal of this volatile, gentle and generous god whom we love and worship. At classical dance recitals of Bharatanatyam, Kuchipudi, Odissi and Mohiniattam, an image of Nataraja is often placed on the stage; the dancers bow and pray to it before beginning the performance. They also often create the Nataraja pose during the dance as they worship the celestial dancer.

FROM TEMPLES TO PALACES

Just like our classical music, many of our classical dances began at the temples. The dancers were called devadasis or the 'handmaiden of God' and they performed before the sanctum as the musicians played their instruments and a singer sang songs. The priests recited mantras and waved lighted lamps and incense before the image. It was part of the ceremony of puja and devadasis were the artists who kept alive our tradition of dance. They were educated women who knew about our religion and its rituals and made the temples a centre of culture. They were like the film stars of today and poets composed songs in praise of their beauty.

Many of our towns and cities grew around an important temple. As a temple grew in popularity, it became larger, and more and more pilgrims would start visiting. Soon a market would grow around the temple and then it would gradually grow into a small town. This is how we have temple towns like Rameswaram,

Dwarka and Puri. Along the road leading off the gates of the temple shops were set up, selling everything from puja material to fruits to saris and food shops welcomed hungry pilgrims. One of the reasons the pilgrims would stay on was to watch the puja rituals and the dance of the devadasis every day. Religion always has a touch of theatre about it because elaborate rituals like *artis*, the drums and flutes and dancers and singers draw people to a temple. They also become centres of crafts, so weavers at temples like those at Varanasi and Kanchipuram began by weaving the saris of the dancers, metal workers made brass arti lamps and incense holders for pujas and potters made plates and bowls for the prasad.

Our dancers always tell a story through their dance—a gift from our storytellers or kathakars. At a time when there were no films or television and as most people could not read or write, everyone waited eagerly for storytellers to come to their village or town and they would find their audience in the courtyard of the temple. Kathakars would tell the stories from our mythology and epics and to make the show more exciting, they would sing and dance to the beat of drums. Our dances began with these storytellers.

Today's dancers combine the roles of a storyteller and a dancer. In kingdoms like Thanjavur and Vijayanagar, the devadasis were respected for their knowledge of literature, music and dance. They were not only well educated but also composed poetry and created new dance routines. They lived in big houses near the temple and held cultural evenings of poetry and music.

The Chola king Raja Raja commissioned the giant Brihadishwara Temple in Thanjavur and the walls are carved with many inscriptions. One inscription lists the devadasis who were employed at the temple and even mentions their salaries.

Soon he kings began to invite them to the palace, where they would perform before the royal family and the nobility. Unlike the dances of the south, the north Indian dance style of Kathak became more of a dance of the royal court of the Mughals in Delhi, the Rajput kingdom of Jaipur and the nawabi city of Lucknow. The last nawab of Lucknow, Wajid Ali Shah, was a well-known poet and even dressed up as Lord Krishna and danced with his courtesans!

DRUMS AND ANKLE BELLS

Classical dance, like our music, also follows the rules laid down in Bharata's Natya Shastra. It is a dazzling blend of movement, music, rhythm and theatre. A single dancer on a stage will play the role of many characters to tell a story. One moment, she is a young Krishna stealing butter and the next she transforms into his mother Yashoda and scolds the boy. A dancer will become the warrior goddess Durga and stride across the stage to kill the asura Mahisha or become soft and gentle Sita living in a forest.

Indian theatre divides emotions into the *navarasas* or nine moods, and a dancer or actor has to know how to express all of them. The navarasas are *shringara* (love); *veer* (valour); *karuna* (pathos); *adbhuta* (wonder); *bhayanaka* (fear); *hasya* (humour); *raudra* (anger) and finally *shanta* (serenity). There will be *abhinaya* or acting as the dancer tells a story just by using the expression on her face and her gestures and body language. And it's not just the expressions that change. There are various styles of dance too. Nritta is pure dance as the dancer moves, sways, bends, leaps and keeps beat with her feet as she dazzles the audience with her speed and variety. Then there is Nritya, which is a mix of abhinaya and nritta. All the movements are carefully choreographed according to the words of the song and the dancer rehearses the performance many times till her dance on stage is flawless.

Today the Sangeet Natak Akademi recognizes eight classical dances performed in different parts of India. These are Bharatanatyam (Tamil Nadu); Kathak (North India); Kuchipudi (Andhra Pradesh); Odissi (Odisha); Sattriya (Assam); Manipuri (Manipur) and Mohiniattam (Kerala). There are also dance theatres like Kathakali of Kerala, Chhau of Chhattisgarh and Yakshagana of Karnataka.

A POLITICIAN HAS MORE
FAKE RASAS THAN
NAVARASAS IN HIS REPERTOIRE.

MOVING FINGERS, FLYING FEET

Of all the classical dances, Bharatanatyam is perhaps the oldest. It developed in the temples of Tamil Nadu, patronized by the temples and the kings. In the beginning, temples were carved out of caves and the Pallava dynasty had built the first free-standing temples made of blocks of stone by the 1st century CE in Mahabalipuram and Kanchipuram, so it probably began there. Over the centuries, the tradition of the dance was becoming lost as people began to disapprove of women who danced. Then, in the 20th century, Rukmini Devi Arundale modernized the dance style. What is performed on stage today, a dazzling blend of dance and theatre, is her creation.

A Bharatanatyam performance is carefully choreographed from the pure dance of the Alarippu to the telling of a story in the varnam and then the dancer takes off in the quicksilver pace of the tillana. The other classical dances are also choreographed similarly, though each section is given a different name. The most fascinating part is the way the dancer uses her lips and eyes to act and her fingers in the *hasta* mudras to tell the story. In this way, they can not just mimic emotions but also show a honeybee flitting over a flower or a running deer. So even if the audience cannot understand the language of the song, the wordless expressions and flying fingers tell the story.

Bharatanatyam, which is the most evolved of the dances with the greatest variety of movements, has 108 *karanas* or movements and poses. We can see them carved on the gopuram gateway of the Shiva temple in Chidambaram, Tamil Nadu. It is a temple dedicated to Nataraja and his dance has been chiselled on stone for all to see. There are thirteen poses just of the head, ten of the body, thirty-six of the eyes, nine of the neck and thirty-seven of the hands and fingers. Perfecting this is the result of years of practice in what is called sadhana or worship.

Kathak was the dance of the royal courts of Delhi, Jaipur and Lucknow, performed before nawabs and maharajas. The costume has a wide skirt, so when the dancer whirls away the dress spreads in a huge circle. The dancers have the choice between wearing a long, full-sleeved and pleated dress called angrakha over tight churidar pyjamas and wearing a ghagra and orhni (dupatta). They wear ghungroos around the ankles and the dance focuses on the feet keeping in rhythm to intricate beats of the tabla, which get faster and faster as the dancer stamps her feet and twirls around the stage.

Kathak comes from the word kathakar and, through movement and acting, the dancer tells a story but there is less use of gestures and facial expressions or the use of the mudras than in Bharatanatyam. Most of the stories that are acted are woven around the legends of Krishna, Radha and the gopis of Vrindavan. In the memoirs of the Mughal emperor Akbar, called Akbarnama, there are miniature paintings of dancers with flaring skirts performing before the king. Drummers and flute players play behind the dancers. So Kathak was already a recognized style of dance at the time of the Mughals.

Kuchipudi was developed in a village of dancers called Kuchipudi in Andhra Pradesh and it borrows many poses and gestures from the older tradition of Bharatanatyam. Kuchipudi was not a temple tradition but more a popular form. Scholars say the name of the village comes from the Sanskrit word kusilava, which means 'a travelling bard or dancer', so the original dancers were folk artists. Artists from Kuchipudi travelled from village to village entertaining people and it has many folk elements to it.

Karnataka also has the folk tradition of Yakshagana, in which dancers wear elaborate masks and headdresses.

Odissi is like Bharatanatyam, it is a dance of the devadasis of the Jagannath Temple in Puri, Odisha. In this dance form, the dancer moves her body, bending and turning in swaying postures. Its typical pose, called *tribhanga*, has the dancer curving her body at the waist and the knee and resembles a palm tree bending in the breeze. Many songs are taken from the 12th century compositions of Jayadeva, a Sanskrit poet, that are about Krishna. The temple dancers were called *maharis* and even boys called *gotipua* danced in the temple. If you look carefully, you'll notice an Odissi dancer in the video for the Michael Jackson song 'Black or White', made in 1991. Do you think Jackson could have done a tribhanga? After all, he was a sensational dancer!

The Mohiniattam dance from Kerala is based on the legend of Mohini, an incarnation of Vishnu and is usually performed by women. The dancer wears a very simple costume—a gold-bordered white sari. Her hair is styled into a huge bun at the side of her head with a garland of flowers around it. Its movements resemble the poses of Bharatanatyam and Kuchipudi, but it is a simpler dance form. In contrast, the Manipuri dancer wears a stiff skirt called *kumil* that dazzles in gold and all the colours of the rainbow. The skirt is so stiff that it sways like a tube as the dancer moves. So, the dance is quite slow and sinuous and as the feet are not visible, all you see are the hands and the face.

A Manipuri dancer who is dancing the female part does not leap or swirl like a Kathak or Odissi dancer would—the more forceful movements of this dance are reserved for the male characters. The themes for most Manipuri routines are taken from the life of Krishna, much like Sattriya.

Sattriya dances from Assam tell the story of Krishna and are based on the Natya Shastra. Earlier, the dancers were all men and so, there were no female characters. Hence, Radha did not appear. Today, Sattriya is performed by men and women clad in Assam's gorgeous muga silk costumes and the male dancers wear a turban.

Bharatanatyam uses drums called mridangams; Kathak dancers tap their feet to the rhythm of the tabla; Sattriya dancers use large, long, curved drums called *khols*. The drummers also dance as they play, leaping and twirling as their long scarves swirl around them.

CAN YOU HEAR THE DRUMS?

We love to dance and sing when we are happy or when we celebrate. Since ancient times, our troupes of folk dancers have travelled from village to village. A village will come out to dance during festivals and celebrations. The tribal people, wearing their majestic headdresses of feather, move so gracefully together. The air turns electric as the drums begin to play, and people gather as singers and musicians fill the air with music. It is quite a show!

In Chhattisgarh and Bengal, Chhau dancers wear masks and bright headdresses and move in a staccato beat, like puppets. In Kerala, Kathakali dancers wear such elaborate make-up that it is hard to believe a human being is dancing before you. Instead of a colourful mask, the face is painted in every colour of the palette—green cheeks and blue foreheads, eyes made to look like giant saucers and red lips. They wear tall headdresses and wide skirts and look like they have stepped out of a fantasy film.

During festivals people have always danced together in our country. In Punjab, they dance the energetic Bhangra and Gidda to the beat of giant dhols (drums). In Gujarat, they click sticks together in a dance called the Dandiya and they dance around in a circle in the Garba, their skirts swirling. In Rajasthan, dancers twirl and circle in majestic, rhythmic movements, wearing silver jewellery, feathers and flowers in the Ghoomar. Naga warriors carry spears and shields in battle dances.

POET, PLAYWRIGHT, GENIUS!

We know that Kalidas was the greatest romantic poet in Sanskrit. His poems like *Meghdutam* and *Ritusamhara* are classics of our literature, but did you know he also wrote plays? Three of his plays have survived: *Abhigyan Shakuntalam*, *Malavikagnimitram* and *Vikram Urvasiyam*. Being in Sanskrit, they have truly teeth-breaking names and here's a challenge, try saying them fast, you are sure to start stammering! One wonders how the actors memorized their lines in Sanskrit.

What is really odd is that even though we know quite a bit about his work, we know hardly anything about Kalidas's life. Unlike most writers who yell out about their books from the rooftops, this great poet-dramatist seems to have been a modest man. He does not talk about himself in any of his works. Reading his poetry and plays very carefully, scholars think that he probably lived in the city of Ujjain, which is an old city from the time before the Mauryas. He lived during the Gupta dynasty, probably during the reign of Chandragupta II as the king was called Vikramaditya and Kalidas mentions the name. Seven of his works have survived, but he may have written more.

Kalidas must have travelled widely in central India because his writing is full of beautiful descriptions of the landscape, rivers, forests and cities of the region. His long poem *Meghdutam* means 'the cloud messenger' and tells the story of a yaksha, a celestial being, who has been banished from heaven by Indra for a year. He misses his wife, who is still living in Swarga. So he sends her a message through a cloud that floats across the land to the Himalayas. Reading the lovely lyrical lines makes you think you are floating in the sky, getting a bird's-eye view of the land.

Here, he is describing a chilly winter in the poem *Ritusamharam*, which describes the six seasons:

'Cold, cold with heavy dews falling thick
And colder yet with the moon beam's icy glitter
Lit with ethereal beauty by wan stars
These nights give no comfort or joy to people'

(Translated by Chandra Rajan)

With storytellers, musicians and dancers, there were many kinds of entertainers—actors, acrobats and magicians. Usually, groups of actors travelled from city to city putting up shows. We still have travelling troupes like the Jatra of Bengal, the Nautanki of Uttar Pradesh and Bihar, Chhau of Odisha, Yakshagana of Karnataka and Kathakali of Kerala. In Tamil, we get a list of words for popular entertainers: a *panar* was a wandering minstrel; a *koothar* was a street performer; a *porunar* was a bard singing battle hymns and a *viraliyar* was a female minstrel.

There were other famous playwrights like Bhasa, who wrote *Svapnavasavadattam*. Sudraka wrote *Mrichhakatikam* (The Little Clay Cart), which was a lively romance. The play is performed even today in Hindi and Girish Karnad based his film *Utsav* on it. As the plays were written mainly in Sanskrit they had long teeth-rattling names. One of Bhasa's plays was named Pratigyanayaugandharayana!

The Natya Shastra describes a play as storytelling through dialogues, action, mime, music, dance, costumes and jewellery. This included *abhinaya*—acting; *angika*—body movement and gestures; *vachika*—words and songs; *aharika*—costumes;

satvika—role playing; *karana*—movement. The first performance was arangetram. So, playing Duryodhana and waving your mace or *gada*, you would do abhinaya and karana. That sounds more exciting than saying act looking fierce, twirling your moustache and stamping your feet.

Unlike Greek theatre, we rarely had very tragic plays as the audience preferred to laugh and have happy endings. There were typical characters like the sutradahar who was a commentator and *vidushak* who was a buffoon. There were even plays that had just one character doing a long monologue. The Natya Shastra also gives clear instructions on how to build a stage. Interestingly, there was a curtain but at the back of the

stage and none in front. The green room, where the actors got
dressed and the singers sat behind this curtain called *yavanika*.
We don't know if they had a prompter to feed lines to actors
who forgot what to say.

To get a taste of the old-style theatre today you can watch a
Ram Leela during Dussehra, where amateur actors perform on
wobbling makeshift stages and you may find Ravana hanging
around at the back smoking a *biri*. In the past, there were no
microphones so actors had to shout, using their hands and facial

expressions in a dramatic way to make themselves understood in the back rows. Some of the mudras of dance were also used by actors so that people who could not hear the dialogues clearly could still get a sense of the story.

The dialogues were a mix of Sanskrit and Prakrit with female characters and poor people speaking in Prakrit and the kings and priests spouting Sanskrit. Women acted in plays in ancient India when there was no purdah, but by medieval times boys were playing the female roles. So, you could play Sita or Draupadi as long as your voice did not break and you did not sprout a moustache!

Bharata does not mention the use of scenery or the use of props but actors used masks like they do in Chhau and even painted their faces like in Kathakali. If you dip into a translation of Kalidas's play *Abhigyan Shakuntalam* it reads pretty much like modern plays. There are dialogues and stage instructions like 'enter a little boy' or 'leave stage from the right'. There are voices that speak off stage and the musicians played away in the background to add to the mood. Many plays must have been written over centuries but only fragments have survived. Won't it be exciting if one could discover a new play by Bhasa or Kalidas written on palm leaves in some dusty corner of an old library? And we'll have a vidushak rolling his eyes and scampering across the stage telling jokes that were written by a genius fifteen hundred years ago.

Six

FARMERS, GARDENERS AND COOKS

Binni, Chuttan and Bishnu knew that the softest, greenest grass could be found in the mango orchard, right in the shade of the mango trees. So that's where they went early every morning and if Dilawar, the head gardener, was not asleep on his charpoy under a tree, then they crept in once again in the evening. Grass was very important to Binni and Chuttan because they were goats and Bishnu, who took care of them and made sure they got the best grass in Lakhi Bagh. Of course, Bishnu did not eat the grass himself. How could he? He was an eight-year-old boy!

In the summer, when the burning hot loo winds blew across the land, the cool shade under these mango trees was Bishnu's favourite place. They said the hotter the loo, the sweeter the mango. As the goats were busy munching the grass, he sat leaning against the thick, gnarly trunk of a mango tree and dreamed, at peace with his world. No one knew he was here. So his older brother Sohan could not tease him, his amma could not make him sweep the courtyard of their hut and his babuji would not growl at him for no reason at all. To avoid them all, this forgotten corner of the orchard was the place to be.

Bishnu looked around happily; there was a cool early morning breeze blowing through the leaves, making a soft swishing sound. A koel was giving its plaintive cry somewhere among the leaves and the fragrance of ripening mangoes made the air smell heavenly. Bishnu had grabbed a dry roti from the kitchen and a handful of fried brinjal and sat eating his impromptu breakfast as the goats ate their grassy meal. Life was good.

That was when he saw a man in a lungi strolling between the trees, looking around him like a visitor. He was a stranger because Bishnu knew all the gardeners who lived and worked in the mango orchard. The man wore a simple cotton sleeveless vest and a white-and-blue chequered lungi and came flapping towards him in leather chappals. He was of medium height, had broad shoulders and walked with a slight limp. As the man got closer, Bishnu saw his moustache drooping downwards around firm lips, large eyes under curved eyebrows and a beaky nose with a small mole next to the left nostril.

Looks like a soldier, Bishnu decided. *What's he doing here?*

By then the man had spotted Bishnu. 'Your goats, are they?' he asked.

Silly question, to whom else could they belong? So Bishnu just nodded.

To his surprise, the man sat down next to him, leant back against the tree trunk, gave a small sigh of happiness and said, 'Ah! It is so peaceful here.'

Bishnu nodded again.

The man turned to study the boy. 'You don't talk much, do you?'

Bishnu shrugged.

'Will you tell me your name, at least?' There was a slight touch of impatience in his voice, just like the way Babuji sounded when Bishnu did not reply to him.

'My name is Bishnu. What's yours?'

The man paused and then said, 'Err . . . Jalal. So, your goats have names too?'

What is wrong with this man? Bishnu wondered, irritated. Of course, his goats had names! How else would he call them?

'That's Binni and the one with the beard is Chuttan.'

'You live in this orchard?'

Bishnu nodded. 'My father is one of the gardeners here.' Then he decided to talk. 'You do know this mango orchard belongs to the king, don't you?'

There was a small smile behind the moustache. 'Yes, I had heard that. It seems the badshah loves mangoes and so he planted this orchard in Darbhanga.'

'Our mangoes are the sweetest in the whole kingdom and the kotwal of Darbhanga and his men will come next month. The gardeners will pick the best mangoes, pack them in straw and put them in wooden boxes. Then he'll send them to our Badshah Akbar in Fatehpur Sikri.'

'The best mangoes in the kingdom, eh?' Jalal sounded doubtful.

'The best!' Bishnu shook his curly head. 'Don't you know this is the famous Lakhi Bagh of Badshah Akbar?'

They fell silent for a while as the man looked around with a happy smile. 'Why is it called Lakhi Bagh?'

'It produces one lakh mangoes, that is why,' Bishnu said with a superior smile.

'One lakh?' Jalal's eyes widened in surprise as he looked around the orchard. 'From one orchard?'

Bishnu shrugged.

'Do you know how many mangoes one lakh amounts to?'

'Not really.' Bishnu had to confess. 'I can only count to twenty.'

Jalal laughed. 'A hundred mangoes a thousand times.'

'Oh!' That sounded like a lot. 'Well, maybe not so many, but they are the sweetest and not because of that silly idea about milk and honey.'

'Silly idea? Milk and honey?' Jalal looked puzzled. 'What do you mean?'

Bishnu scrambled up and looked to a tree that had some low-hanging mangoes. He jumped up and plucked one. Peeling it with a small knife that he carried in his kurta pocket, he offered a slice to Jalal.

'Tell me, is it sweet or not?'

Jalal chewed and gave a huge smile. 'Ah! Perfect!'

'Now some stupid hakim in Agra has told the badshah that he should pour milk and honey on the roots of the trees to make the fruit sweeter.'

Jalal frowned. 'That is stupid?'

'Of course! If I pour karela juice on the roots, will the mangoes turn bitter? Will lemon juice make them sour?'

'Of course not!' They sat happily chewing away. 'Stupid idea.'

'Everyone at the orchard is laughing at the order,' Bishnu said, after a thoughtful pause.

'So no one will pour milk and honey on the roots?'

'Of course they won't! Amma says we will drink the milk and she'll make besan ladoos with the honey.'

'Good idea!' Jalal agreed. 'Why waste them on trees?' And the two of them shared an understanding smile.

Jalal got up and said with a sigh, 'Now I have to get ready for work.'

'You are a soldier, no?' Bishnu asked and Jalal nodded. 'You use a sword or a spear?'

THEY ARE FOR YOU
AND YOUR FRIENDS.

'Oh, a sword!'

By the time he replied, Bishnu had already climbed up to a
low branch to pluck two mangoes. He handed them to his new
friend. 'They are for you and your friends . . .'

'Oh, thank you, Bishnu!'

With a wave, the Mughal emperor Jalaluddin Akbar walked
away with his mangoes, thinking that his friend Birbal would
enjoy the story of the milk and honey.

~~~~~

The Mughal emperor Akbar was very fond of mangoes and did plant a huge orchard in Darbhanga, Bihar. People claimed it was named Lakhi Bagh as it had one lakh mango trees. Also that at the orders of the king, gardeners poured milk and honey on the roots of his favourite trees. These are just stories, one hundred thousand trees or even a harvest of one lakh mangoes is a wild exaggeration and so is the story of milk and honey but then again, Indians have always liked to talk big and exaggerate.

In this chapter, you will meet the farmers and gardeners who have filled our kitchens with a cornucopia of grains, cereals, vegetables, spices and fruits. We know about great chefs and our many cuisines, but what would we do without our farmers and gardeners? Can you imagine sitting down to a meal without their generosity?

FROM VILLAGES TO CITIES

A civilization is the culture and history of a land—its literature, crafts, religion, architecture, music, art and even food. A civilization begins with the cities, but we would have no cities without our villages and farmers. As a matter of fact, civilizations begin with the growing of two food items: wheat and rice. Humans were first hunter-gatherers as tribes of people wandered from place to place looking for the food they could gather from forests—fruits, berries, edible grasses, honey and herbs. This gathering was usually done by the women as the men went hunting for deer and wild boar. Then they would eat the forest produce and the animals after cooking over an open fire.

Some smart men and women in Mesopotamia realized that seeds from wild grasses grew once again when they fell

on earth. So, they began to plant the seeds and water them and that was the beginning of agriculture. Soon, they had stopped wandering, built huts and begun to grow regular crops of grains, fruits and vegetables. So, we have to thank these people of Mesopotamia for our civilizations. Agriculture first began by the banks of the rivers Tigris and Euphrates in the area of Iraq, Syria and Jordan, which was called Mesopotamia. In Egypt, it began by the banks of the River Nile and in India by the River Indus. This is the Agricultural Revolution and without it there would be no villages or cities, just hunter-gatherers wandering around in forests.

Soon, farmers were growing more than they could eat and so they began to barter their crops. Sometimes they'd go to the potter and say, 'I'll give you a basket of barley in exchange for a water pot.' As they began trading with people from other villages, a marketplace sprang up where craftspeople began selling pottery and cloth. Then clever priests built a small temple and soon a town would grow around the temple with regular shops. As a town grew with kings and priests, craftspeople and musicians, it became a city and life in the cities is a civilization.

The cities do not grow food. Everything from cereals, grains, vegetables, spices, fruits to milk, butter, sugar and ghee come from the villages. In exchange, the cities provide everything from clothes and cars to mobile phones and medicines. Villages can survive without cities, but without our farmers our cities would die. In India, Persia and China, apart from wheat and

barley, the main crop has been rice and our first cities of the Indus Valley Civilization—Mohenjo-daro and Harappa—were surrounded by villages growing wheat, rice, barley and millet.

So, whether you are sitting down to have dinner or buying a sari, remember to thank our farmers and gardeners. Our culture is a gift of our villages.

HAVE AN AMRA, PLEASE!

We all hate summer and pray for rain, but there is the dilemma—if the hot loo winds don't blow, the mangoes won't ripen. Then you get no mango chutney, no mango slices in vanilla ice cream, no mango juice dripping over your chin, no aam papar, no aam panna or mango milkshake. So, the whole country grits its teeth and looks to the golden prize at the end of the hot summer tunnel—mangoes!

In most countries, gardeners save their most poetic names for flowers, but in India they get dreamy over a fruit—the mango! There is a mango called Begum Pasand or 'the favourite of the begums'; Himsagar, like an icy sea; and Golap Khas, like a rose. They say one variety was named Langra because it was created by a lame fakir from Varanasi and there is even an obscure variety named after the bitter gourd called Karela because it has a bitter aftertaste.

Here is a short list of some of the popular varieties of Indian mangoes: Dussehri, Alphonso, Rataul, Safeda, Husn-e-ara, Pairi, Sindhu, Mallika, Samar Bahisht, Avalla, Suvarnarekha, Totapuri, Chausa, Zafran, Badami, Moovandan, Banganpalli... and we are only getting started! All of them are grown by patient gardeners who transformed one mango variety into many through years of experimenting with them. What really happened was that through centuries, thousands of mango growers experimented with taste, texture and colour and created hundreds of varieties of mangoes through careful grafting. Mangoes now come in many shapes and sizes—round, oval, kidney or heart shaped—and colours like green, yellow and even touched with red. There are two main types—the firm-fleshed mangoes and the ones with a thinner texture, filled with juice that mango lovers suck straight from the fruit. At a rough count, there are over a thousand varieties of mangoes in India and the number keeps growing.

The mango is an Indian fruit that we gifted to the world and its Latin name proves it—*Mangifera indica*. Botanists tell us that it is a member of the cashew family and the original wild mango variety originated in the Himalayan foothills of north-east India, close to Myanmar. Though if you ask any mango grower from Malihabad to Ratnagiri, they'll tell you with great aplomb that the first mangoes in the world were grown by his great-great-great-great-grandfather and he grew it right here in this orchard, on that tree in the corner, where the goats are grazing.

The Mughal kings, especially Akbar, were connoisseurs of mangoes and patronized many orchards like Lakhi Bagh. The nawabs of Murshidabad had special knives made of bamboo so that the mango flesh would not get bruised when they were sliced. The Mahabharata mentions a meat dish cooked with mangoes.

In the north, the mango is called *aam* and it is a simplification of the Sanskrit word *amra*. The Tamil word is *mankai* or *mangai* and the Portuguese, who picked Tamil names for many foods, turned it into *manga*. By the time it entered the English language, it had become mango. If you look around, mangoes are everywhere as every village has its

YEAH, SURE!

WORLD'S FIRST-EVER
MANGO TREE. MY
GREAT-GREAT-GREAT
GREAT-GRANDFATHER
PLANTED IT.

mango orchard. Rows of auspicious mango leaves are strung into garlands and sway over a doorway to welcome guests. During all pujas, five mango leaves on a branch are placed in a copper pot of Ganga water as the *kalash* placed before the image of a deity. One of the favourite motifs of weavers and textile printers is the curving, mango-shaped ambi, which the English call paisley. Bharatanatyam dancers wear the mangamalai necklace, made of tiny gold mangoes.

And the mango tree is called a *kalpavriksha* or 'tree of life' and is considered sacred as it brings good fortune.

Indians often get all hot and bothered about mangoes and the hottest argument is about the great north–south mango divide. Which is the king of mangoes? North Indians vote for the slim, golden, ambrosial Dussehri grown in the orchards of Malihabad in Uttar Pradesh. People from the Deccan, especially Goa and Maharashtra, drool over the subtle flavours of the Alphonso grown in the orchards of Ratnagiri. Then the arguments heat up as the Biharis declare that you can't beat the Langra of Madhubani and Bengal only wants the Himsagar. If you ask me, no mango can beat the taste of the Dussehri, the favourite of the nawabs of Awadh—sweet, creamy and with a mellow rosy flavour. I find the Alphonso bland, the Langra stringy and the Himsagar too mild. Let the battle begin!

QUITE A LEAF!

Betel, paan, *tambula, beeda, killi, gilori* . . . that's a lot of names for a leaf. Tamils love it so much they call it *vetrilai* or *vetthile*, meaning 'truly a leaf'. In Sanskrit, it is called *parna*, which simply means 'a leaf'. We chew it smeared with kattha or catechu paste, a spot of lime and slices of areca nuts and we think chewing paan is unique to the Indian subcontinent. It is not. We learnt to chew paan from South East Asian countries like Cambodia and Vietnam, from where Indian sailors picked up the habit.

The most cheerful shop in a market is a paan shop, noisy with conversation as the radio plays film music or cricket commentary. The smiling paanwallah sits before a large brass bowl in which a stack of heart-shaped leaves are kept wrapped in a wet red cloth. There are rows of bowls, jars and bottles filled with colourful pastes and powders; a brass bowl of lime; and an array of spoons and spatulas. In our society, a paanwallah is a very important person as they serve up news and gossip while folding a paan and they also listen to you. With lightning speed, a leaf is taken out, the stalk broken off, a smear of lime paste and another of the brown kattha. Then the customer selects from an aromatic choice of ingredients—areca nut, cardamom, camphor, coconut powder, candied fruit, fennel seeds and a rose jam called gulkand. The leaf is swiftly folded into a triangle and a clove stuck in to hold it together; you open your mouth wide and chew, and if you are so inclined, you spit a disgusting red stream of juice.

This aromatic, heart-shaped leaf grows on the betel vine, the *Piper betle*, and it belongs to the pepper family. The earliest reference to the chewing of paan can be found in a Vietnamese text. The supari or areca nut, which is essential for making a paan, was first grown in Malaysia. It is the nut of a palm tree and not the betel vine, though it is mistakenly also called a betel nut. The city of Varanasi is the undisputed paan capital of India, where everyone from shopkeepers and rickshawallahs to housewives and policemen have reddened lips and stained teeth. They have a separate bazaar for paan where the variety of leaves arrive from all across India. The most expensive is the pale green Maghai grown around Patna. The other varieties like Bangla, Venmony, Tirur, Mahoba, Sanchi, Kapoori, Dasavari and Ambari have colours ranging from a pale lemon to a dark green.

Like the French make a huge theatre out of drinking wine, we Indians like to show off our knowledge of paan. The paan boxes can be made of brass or silver and the nutcrackers used to slice the areca nut have pretty handles in the shape of peacocks and parrots. Even the lowly spittoons in which the nawabs spat paan juice were made of silver. Delicately embossed silver plates were used to offer paan to guests after a meal, ceremoniously made by a begum or a maharani. And of course, in those days we did not have lipsticks, so young women chewed paan to redden their lips.

There are stories of rich nawabs adding ground pearls, musk and zarda to their paan. Zarda are globules of tobacco dipped in aromatic oils and covered in silver leaf. If you are not used to it, a zarda-laced paan can make your head spin. The ancient practitioners of Ayurveda and Unani medicine—the vaids and hakims—approved of chewing paan. Consuming it is said to relieve cough, while the juice helps with arthritic pain, heals wounds and is a tonic, when mixed with honey. Even our films can't resist singing about paan. A delightful Waheeda Rehman sang of her lover chewing paan and staining his kurta, 'Paan khaye saaiyan hamaro!', and Amitabh Bachchan, in the song 'Khaike Paan Banaraswala', claimed it opens the locks of your mind. It really is a very special leaf.

A WILD GRASS? REALLY!

It is one of the eternal images of our villages. When travelling by train, we have all loved the scene of the deep emerald green of paddy fields going past the window with rows of men and women bending and replanting the rice saplings. If you asked a botanist to describe rice, they would say it is the seeds of a wild aquatic grass. That doesn't sound like the grain that is the main staple diet of more than half the world's population, does it? But then our farmers took a look at a grass and with great patience and ingenuity, turned a wild grass into rice. As early as 10,000 BCE, they were growing rice on the terraced fields of Kashmir. From pulao to dosa, appam to chiwda, puttu to murukku and khichdi, what would we do without rice?

Around ten million years ago, a huge landmass broke up. One bit became Africa, the other India and the third was Australia. This land mass was called Gondwanaland and on it grew a wild grass that people learnt to cultivate. Its seeds were covered by brown husks that had to be taken off and inside were the grains that were boiled and eaten. In India, we first grew a variety called *Oryza sativa* and from it, thousands of types have been cultivated—long grained and short grained—in various colours, like white, cream, brown, red and even black. There were no agricultural scientists in the past, so it was all the work of our quiet farmers who experimented and created many varieties of rice.

Many countries in Asia claim to have started the cultivation of rice. China says it began in the Pearl River Valley; Indian archaeologists have found remains of rice at their digs in the Indo-Gangetic plains; botanists have spotted the wild grass in the north-eastern states of India, while Bangladesh and Myanmar and Vietnam also grew rice very early. China-India-Myanmar is called the rice triangle and no one can really know for certain where it began, but does it really matter?

Unlike grains like barley and millet, rice is not an easy crop to grow. It needs a lot of water as an aquatic grass and a paddy field has to be flooded with water. The seedlings are first grown in one spot and then replanted in the main field. The farmer has to keep a careful watch over the level of water and when they grow rice in the hills, the sides of the hills are cut into terraced fields in beautiful layers that look like a giant hand carved them out of rock. In this way, rainwater would be trapped on the terraces. The first Aryans probably did not know of rice as it is not mentioned in the first book, the Rig Veda, but it appears in the second book, the Yajur Veda.

Usually, there are two crops harvested in winter and summer, of which the winter crop, called Shali, is considered superior. During the time of the Mauryan dynasty, a variety called Mahashali was grown only for the royal family. Nowadays, the most popular rice is called basmati, though it is not one of our traditional varieties. It was brought to India by a former king of Afghanistan called Amir Dost Mohammad Khan as late as 19th century CE. He was banished to the Dehradun region by the British when they colonized Afghanistan and his farmers began to grow the long-grained and fragrant basmati rice that is now enjoyed across the world. Many chefs declare that the best biryani and pulao is made with basmati rice, but the nawabs of Lucknow and the Mughals of Delhi and Agra who first encouraged these dishes never tasted the basmati. Neither did Emperor Ashoka ever have a basmati khichri.

We love to argue about food and there are two arguments that never die down and both dishes use rice. First, which is older: the dosa or the idli? Second, which rice preparation is superior: the pulao of Lucknow or the biryani of Delhi? Chefs from the town of Udupi popularized dosa and idli in the rest of India. The round pillowy balls of idlis are perfect for breakfast and the crisp pancake of the dosa for lunch makes everyone happy. We are all familiar with them eaten with the accompaniment of sambar, coconut and tomato chutney and the super spicy dal powder called podi or as we say, with a sniff and a gasp, gunpowder!

The variety of dosas shows the talent of southern cooks. They can be plain or stuffed with a filling made of onions and potatoes or cottage cheese or even minced meat. It takes a lot of practice to fry a perfect dosa; a mix of urad dal and rice is ground and then fermented overnight and this batter is shallow fried in a perfect circle. In Tamil Nadu, the dosa is thick, spongy and small. In Karnataka, it is large, thin and crunchy. A similar batter is steamed to make the idli. To look for the history of a dish, you have to look in books and there were many recipe books written for the rulers of kingdoms. The dosa is mentioned first in the 6th century BCE in Tamil Sangam literature, but the idli finds mention in Kannada literature only four centuries later. Someone wrote a poem in praise of the dosa 2500 years ago!

The great food historian K.T. Achaya said that the Hindu kings of Bali in Indonesia often came to South India in search of brides. They probably brought a traditional Balinese dish called kedli, which was made by fermenting soya bean, fish and groundnut, grinding them into a paste and then steaming. Indian cooks picked up the art of steaming a fermented paste from them, used rice and dal instead and produced the idli. Kerala has a famous version called the Ramassery idli that is made by only four families of the Mudaliar community in the Ramassery village in Palakkad district. The thin, delicate idli is steamed through a muslin cloth and leaves placed on top of an earthen pot. No stainless steel idli makers here.

The idli may have had an Indonesian origin but we are pretty sure biryani originated in Persia, where rice is called birinj. Most of us would find it difficult to find the difference between a pulao and a biryani as both have rice and meat cooked together with a magical blend of spices. The process of cooking a biryani is called dum pukht, in which layers of saffron-drenched rice and cooked meat are steamed in a handi sealed with dough. Our oldest texts mention three rice dishes—payodana, rice mixed with yoghurt and ghee, which would be our curd rice; kshiradana, rice boiled in milk and honey that we still have as kheer; and mamsadana or rice cooked with meat, which is our pulao. The parmanna, payesam, payesh, whatever we call it, is first mentioned in Buddhist and Jain literature as early as 400 BCE, so we have been dipping our spoons into bowls of payesh for 2400 years!

NO CHICKEN CURRY?

In India, some vegetarians make a lot of noise about their diet being the best one, but you will be surprised to know that a government survey says only around 29 per cent of Indians are strict vegetarians. While about 75 per cent of Rajasthan and 61 per cent of Gujarat are vegetarians, only 1.7 per cent of Telangana and 2 per cent of Nagaland are vegetarian and around 1.6 per cent of the people of Bengal will refuse a fish fry. In Lakshadweep, you might not find a vegetarian at all!

It is declared by people munching vegetables with a holier-than-thou expression that the religion of the Aryans that we call Hinduism believes in a vegetarian diet. Is that true? We have to check the Vedas and Upanishads to find out what they ate in ancient India. The ancient religion of the Vedas was a sacrificial one. It meant performing a fire ritual called yagna and that often meant the sacrifice of animals to the gods. The cooks then prepared a big feast with the sacrifice, which everyone including the priest enjoyed. Some sources say that at least fifty types of meats are listed in the ancient books as being fit for sacrifice, but for some strange reason, chicken and eggs were not allowed.

Yagnas were not just expensive but also cruel as kings and noblemen would sacrifice hundreds of animals during the rituals as a show of wealth. The reformers Gautama Buddha and Vardhaman Mahavira decided to reject the idea of animal sacrifice. From their teachings, especially those of Mahavira, the tradition of vegetarianism began. So, vegetarianism did not start as a Hindu tradition at all. The Jains believe that every form of life, from a bumblebee to an elephant, is sacred and they believe in ahimsa or non-violence towards all living creatures. Some Jain monks and nuns are so strict in their faith that they walk barefoot so they don't step on any organisms and wear masks so that they don't breathe them in.

The Mauryan king Chandragupta became a Jain, while his grandson Ashoka became a Buddhist. Many Hindu philosophers like Shankara, Madhava and Ramanuja followed in their footsteps and changed the rules of yagnas to replace animals with fruits and vegetables as offerings. That is why now devotees carry a puja thali with coconuts and bananas and slice up pumpkins and gourds after smearing them with turmeric. It is a much kinder sacrifice, it is cooked as prasad and everyone has a great vegetarian meal. Today, it's only the Brahmins of Bengal and Kashmir and the Saraswat Brahmins of Maharashtra who don't practise vegetarianism, whereas the clever Bengalis declare that fish are a crop of the sea! To eat meat or not to do so should be a personal choice. The Mughal emperor Akbar became a vegetarian, but he did not stop his friend Abul Fazl from serving biryani and mutton korma.

What do the physicians of Ayurveda say about an all-vegetarian diet, you ask? Both Charaka and Sushruta say a balanced diet is essential for good health and not only do they recommend meat and fish, they also suggest we drink some wine. In their books, no diet is completely vegetarian. They recommend a meat diet to gain energy and to recover from illness. Of course, they also suggest you eat peacocks and crocodiles!

Our vegetarian recipes are the most varied in the world and they show the imagination and cleverness of our cooks. They use herbs and spices with ingenuity and keep using newer ingredients, just as our farmers keep experimenting and

growing newer varieties of crops. We learnt to grow oranges, pears, lettuce and cinnamon from the Chinese. The Portuguese introduced potatoes, tomatoes, green chilli, capsicum, cashew nuts, cocoa and kidney beans that they brought from the Americas. Our farmers began to grow them and then our chefs and home-cooks, that is, our mothers and fathers, used an inspired mix of herbs and spices to create unique dishes. Take our samosa, it is not an Indian dish at all. The Arabs brought the samusak—a triangle of fried dough stuffed with minced meat. Indian cooks replaced the meat with spicy potatoes, which came with the Portuguese, and using Indian spices like garam masala, we got the samosa!

SHAH JAHAN HAS LUNCH

Today we have famous chefs in restaurants and television programmes, but in medieval times, they were found in palace kitchens. Some of the finest chefs worked in the Mughal kitchens of Delhi and Agra and the Nawabi ones of Lucknow and Hyderabad. That is how we got the menu of biryani, pulao, kababs, korma, kalia and many kinds of delicious desserts. We have a description of a meal served to the Mughal emperor Shah Jahan. He usually ate in the harem and the dishes arrived from all the kitchens in the fortress. So the king would sit down to anywhere up to fifty dishes placed on the carpet called the *dastarkhwan*. The khansama would describe each dish and the king would pick the ones he would eat and the rest would be given to the harem women for their meal.

In many royal households, the recipes were written down and these ancient manuscripts have been found at palaces over time. One such collection is called *Nuskha-e-Shahjahani* and has many rich and complex dishes. All the chefs competed to capture Shahjahan's attention and they created really original dishes. There are meat kormas using mangoes, oranges, melons and even bitter gourd. One dish named Aash-e-Nakhudi needed twenty-one very expensive ingredients, including rare spices. Did you know that sambar was first created at the court of the Maratha kings of Thanjavur?

The talent of our bakers can be shown by the long list of breads they produce. We have baati, bhakri, bhatura, kulcha, lachhe, rumali, naan, poori, taftan, phefra, rotli, do patri and sheermal. Rotis can be plain or tandoori, khameeri, makki, missi . . . then fried in ghee for many kinds of paratha. In the north, the poori is made with atta; in Bengal, it is made with maida and called luchi. One thing puzzles me—what is the difference between a roti, chappati and phulka? Or are they the same? Because they all taste just delectable!

The menus of kings were planned by the royal physicians, the vaids and hakims. The Mughal and Nawabi kitchens were huge establishments. Each kitchen was headed by a Mir Bakawal, who supervised everything. The selected dishes to be sent to the king were put in sealed containers, tied up in cloth with the name of the cook written on it. A procession of dishes was then carried by the khansama and taken to the harem, where they were first tasted for poison and then served to the king and princes. Shah Jahan's meal was always supervised by his daughter Jahanara, who was the head of the harem.

The cooks of large kitchens were called *bawarchis* and the gourmet chef was called *rakabdar* as he only cooked very small amounts to serve on a small plate called *rakabi*. The *abdar* was responsible for the drinking water and all liquid refreshments like sherbets and fruit juices. The *masalchi*'s job was to grind the masalas and the *kababchi* only made kababs. At the bottom of the list was the *degshor*, who washed all the pots and pans, including the giant cooking pots called *degs*. If the king liked a dish from that kitchen, a small bag of coins would be sent and shared everyone and maybe even with the poor degshor would get a mohur or two.

Seven

MERCHANTS, SAILORS AND PILGRIMS

Basava and his elder sister Sundari sat on the sand watching the sun rise over the sea. Slowly, the sky turned from grey to blue and the edges of the clouds were touched with orange and pink. They sat staring at the horizon, that line in the distance where the bowl of the sky seemed to curve down to meet the sea.

Their father was a sailor who had sailed away on a merchant ship many months ago and they were eagerly waiting for him to come home. So, every morning at sunrise, they came and waited by the beach, hoping to see the tall red sails of their father's ship rise slowly above the horizon. They had seen many ships come and go as they lived in Mamallapuram, which was a busy port. The ships came from many distant lands, carrying exciting cargo—chests of silk and pottery, jars full of wine and even horses. Their father's ship had sailed out carrying logs of sandalwood, woven cloth, spices and ghee.

'It's been so many months,' Sundari said with a sigh. 'Appa has never been away for so long.'

'Remember the big storm last week?' Basava added worriedly. 'The sea was full of high waves. I hope Appa's ship is safe.'

'Look! A ship is coming!' Sundari stood up in excitement. 'But I can't see the sails.'

As they watched eagerly, a ship appeared on the horizon like a dot that grew larger as it came closer. The sails filled with wind and they saw the high masts and the wooden bow.

'No,' Basava whispered in disappointment. 'Appa's ship has red sails with a flying eagle painted on them. This one has black and green sail.'

Disheartened, the children headed for home. They had work to do. The money their father had left for them when he went on his voyage had run out, as it always happened after a while. Their amma sold vegetables in the market, so that they had enough to eat, and the two children would help. In the morning, they would set up the stall and their amma would join them after cooking lunch.

Sundari liked working at the vegetable stall. The market was an interesting place. Often, their customers were sailors from different lands—some with pale skin and narrow eyes and others with dusky skin and curly hair. They wore odd clothes and jewellery and spoke in languages she could not understand at all!

This morning, as Basava was laying out the bundles of spinach and piles of brinjals, pumpkins and gourds, one of their regular customers came to buy vegetables. She was the wife of a merchant who owned many ships. She knew all about the ships coming and going from Mamallapuram.

As she picked through the radishes and beans, she asked, 'Any news of your father?' When Sundari shook her head sadly, she said, 'Why don't you go and ask at the jetty where all the ships are anchored.'

'Ask what?' Basava leaned forwards eagerly.

'Ask the sailors if they have seen your father's ship on the way to Mamallapuram. My husband does that quite often when his ships are late.'

That afternoon, the children headed towards the main jetty. They went through the market and took the street going towards the sea. They went past warehouses where merchants kept goods meant to be loaded into ships. In one warehouse, labourers were unloading bags of pepper and coriander seeds. In another, they were stacking up bales of cotton cloth woven in bright colours.

Three ships stood anchored at the jetty, tied to the shore with thick ropes. Two more ships were waiting out at sea, ready to come in. Small boats were moving in and out among the ships, selling everything from fruits and flowers to beads and woodcarvings. Among the ships anchored at the jetty was the ship with the black and green sails that they had seen that morning.

As they went past a ship being loaded with goods, a soldier carrying a spear stopped them. 'Halt! Watch where you are going!' the man yelled. 'No one is allowed on this ship without a royal permit.'

'Permit?' Sundari looked puzzled. 'Why?'

'Because it is a royal ship, you silly girl!'

'You mean this ship belongs to the royal navy?' Basava's eyes widened in surprise. 'Are we going to war?'

'Of course not! This is a trading ship. His Majesty King Narasimha Varman owns many ships that trade with far-off kingdoms. This one is going to the port of Tamralipti in the north.'

'We are looking for a ship that has come from the kingdom of Kamboja . . .' Sundari began hesitantly. 'Our father is a sailor and he sailed for Kamboja many months ago. We want to ask the sailors if they saw his ship.'

'Kamboja?' the soldier asked. He then pointed to the ship with the black and green sail and said kindly, 'That ship arrived from there.'

They ran to the ship, up the gangplank and on to its deck. They stopped when they saw that all the sailors on board were foreigners and were speaking to each other in a different language.

'Oh no!' Basava said with a sigh. 'How do we make them understand us?'

'Easy!' Sundari grinned. 'We talk to them like Amma does when they come to buy vegetables.'

'Of course!' laughed Basava. 'We act and make signs with our hands.'

They looked around trying to spot someone with a friendly face. Finally, they went up to a sailor sitting on a roll of rope. He was an old man with a dark, leathery, sunburnt face and deep lines around his narrow eyes. He wore loose pyjamas, a sleeveless jacket, silver bangles and earrings.

'Kamboja?' Sundari asked nervously.

The man nodded happily. 'Kamboja!'

Basava pointed to the sail, then pointed to the red skirt Sundari was wearing and asked, 'Ship? Red sail?'

The man frowned and shook his head.

Sundari tried to explain. She tapped the side of the ship and said, 'Ship?' The man nodded as if he understood. Then she pointed to the sail and to her skirt. 'Red sail?'

The man pointed to the sea and said something in his own language.

'Our father . . . Appa!' Basava was acting out a tall man with a moustache.

The man flapped his arms to mimic a bird flying.

'YES! YES!' the children jumped and yelled in delight. 'There is a flying eagle on the red sails!'

The man laughed as he stood up and pulled them by their hands to the other end of the ship. Then he pointed to the horizon, where a ship was slowly sailing towards them, its red sails blowing proudly in the breeze.

Basava and Sundari were speechless! There before their eyes were the familiar high masts, the curving prow shaped like a peacock, the red sails with the flying eagles . . .

'Your appa is a sailor?' the man asked gently, looking at their delighted faces. 'Is he on that ship?'

'Oh!' They stared at the man in disbelief.

'You can speak our language!' Sundari exclaimed.

'A little bit,' said the man, laughing. 'I come to Mamallapuram often. But I did enjoy your acting, especially, the "tall man with a moustache" bit!'

Then Basava, Sundari and their new friend stood by the sea, happily watching one more ship come home.

~~~~~~

Basava and Sundari's father was coming home from modern Cambodia and even today, the children of sailors and fishermen stand by the seashore and wait anxiously for the ships and boats to come home. Basava and Sundari knew how dangerous a sailor's life could be. Not only were there storms at sea but also the fear of pirates who raided merchant ships. It was the merchants carrying goods by road and sea who made India prosperous. It began with the Indus Valley Civilization trading with Mesopotamia and Egypt. Then our textiles and spices were taken across West Asia to the Roman Empire and the rich ladies of Rome were wearing the muslins woven in Bengal and their cooks were adding pepper and turmeric to their dishes.

THE MERCHANT LORDS

From the time of the Buddha, we have stories about rich businessmen and wealthy craftspeople. There was a potter named Saddalaputta who employed 500 potters in what can only be called a factory and also owned a fleet of boats. Another merchant named Anathapindika gifted the Buddha

with a mango grove and legend has it that he covered the ground with gold coins. From the time of the Mauryans, craftspeople and merchants began to convert to Buddhism and Jainism because they did not like being treated as lower castes by the Brahmins and Kshatriyas. Just as the farmers and craftspeople, who were called shudras, the merchants, categorized as Vaishyas, were tired of being taxed and exploited by those in power. When two of our greatest religious reformers and teachers, Gautama Buddha and Vardhaman Mahavira, rejected the caste system, lots of merchants became Buddhists and Jains and began supporting monasteries.

Merchants and craftspeople were organized into guilds. The guilds got the orders from customers, fixed wages and controlled prices. They also gave loans, donated to monasteries and helped build stupas and viharas. In the north, the guilds were called Srenis and in the south, Chettis.

The Chettiyars of Tamil Nadu owned ships and took goods across the Indian Ocean to Myanmar, Malaya, Vietnam and Indonesia. Many settled in these countries, built temples and influenced the life, culture and religion of the people. They would lend money to the kings and build luxurious mansions with walls and ceilings covered in expensive Burmese teak. They also developed a new cuisine influenced by the food they tasted on their travels called Chettinad cuisine. To help trade, the Chola kings sent three embassies to the court of the Chinese kings. It is recorded by the Chinese that in 105 CE the Tamils gifted the Chinese king 21,000 ounces of pearls, sixty elephant tusks and a precious perfume called frankincense. The Pandyan kings sent emissaries to the Byzantine court at Constantinople.

BATTLE AT SEA

The Cholas ruling in the Tamilakam kingdom were a great marine power. Their ships took off from the Cholamandalam Coast from ports like Kaveripattinam and Poompuhar. The kings of the Chera dynasty of Kerala had ports at Cochin, Calicut and Muziris along the Malabar Coast. These ports were cosmopolitan places with Chinese, Arabs, Jews, Persians and Malays wandering about the markets and mosques, synagogues and churches beside the temples. Our ships were very unusual because they were built without any nails, since ships built with nails broke easily in a storm. Instead, planks of wood were cut in the shape of the ship and then tied tightly with strong ropes. The best sailors, however, were Arabs, who had discovered the patterns of the monsoon winds that blew like clockwork around India and they used this to sail along the Arabian Sea. Many Arabs settled in Kerala and married local women. Their descendants are called the Mappilas.

The Chola navy provided armed escorts for the merchant ships of the Chettiyars. In 1025 CE Rajendra Chola fought with the kingdom of Srivijaya in the Malacca Straits, which is the sea between Malaysia and Indonesia, and it was the only time that an Indian king fought a naval battle. Ships on the way to China would stop at Srivijaya to stock up on food and water, but they were taxed heavily and the kings allowed pirates to attack the ships. In retaliation, an armada of ships of the Chola navy attacked and looted the Srivijaya capital of Palembang. Their king was captured and brought back to Tamilakam and the famous jewelled gates of Palembang called the Vidyadhara Torana were also taken away. Rajendra Chola was so proud of his victory that he carved his exploits on the walls of the Brihadishwara Temple in Thanjavur.

Indian culture and religion influenced life in countries from Myanmar to Indonesia. The kings had Sanskrit names and one of the titles of the king of Thailand is Rama even today. The people are familiar with the Ramayana and their traditional dances and music are woven around the epic. The temples of Angkor Wat in Cambodia and Borobudur in Indonesia have carvings of the Buddha and Hindu gods and goddesses. India's cultural influence through trade was peaceful, unlike the European traders who chose violence, colonized and exploited the people for centuries.

A CARAVAN TO SAMARKAND

Goods travelled by road across India and the Mauryans had built a network of well-made roads to improve trade. The Dakshinapatha, 'the road going south', began in Pataliputra and ended at the Gujarat ports of Bharukachha and Surat. One branch of the Dakshinapatha went southwards towards the Deccan. Another was the Uttarapatha, 'the road going north' that started in Pataliputra, went through north India to join

I TOLD YOU SO!

UTTARAPATHA

IF YOU ARE HERE, THEN YOU ARE DEFINITELY LOST!

DAKSHINAPATHA

the Silk Roads, eventually weaving through central Asia. This road still exists and we call it the Grand Trunk Road and instead of bullock carts and camels, we have loaded trucks lumbering along.

As these journeys took months to complete, merchants were often accompanied by their families, so a large group would travel together. One Buddhist Jataka tale describes a caravan of one thousand bullock carts. They hired armed guards and guides called *sarthavaha* and as the roads were rough and bumpy, the merchants would travel very slowly, sometimes stopping at inns. The roads went through jungles and deserts, and there were wild animals and criminal tribes who attacked travellers. So being a merchant was not easy.

No merchants travelled from India all the way to Rome. Goods changed hands many times along the Silk Roads that connected China to Rome. The caravans would travel through Afghanistan, Iran, Iraq, the Middle East to reach the Red Sea, cross over to Egypt and then go on to Venice and Rome. Along the way would be legendary cities like Taxila, Bukhara, Samarkand, Babylon, Damascus and Baghdad, which were great cultural centres with philosophers, poets, mathematicians and astronomers working there. Many Indians lived there, like the scientists and astronomers patronized by the caliph of Baghdad. We hear of Indian astrologers working in Alexandria and Rome.

It was not just goods that travelled along the Silk Roads, but ideas too. Buddhism was taken to China and beyond by monks from Buddhist universities like Nalanda. The Indian numerical system was carried by Arab merchants to Europe. This was also a road for pandemics. Diseases like a plague called Black Death was carried by travellers along this road. There was one trade that people don't talk about—slaves. All the cities had

slave markets and humans were bought and sold like goods. There were no cargo planes or oil tankers, but this was also globalization of another kind.

A PILGRIM'S TRAIL

With the merchants, there was another kind of traveller on the roads—the pilgrims. We know of Chinese pilgrims like Hsuan Tsang and Fa Hian who wrote about India, but the maximum number of pilgrims were Indians, many of them sadhus. They would walk for months and months to reach pilgrimage spots called tirthas, walking along narrow hill paths to pray at Kedarnath and the cave of Amarnath. Others would cross forests and deserts, wade through rivers and face adverse weather to cross a land.

The pilgrim trails are called yatras and people walked and covered huge distances. The Sapta Puri yatra was to seven sacred cities of Varanasi, Haridwar, Ayodhya, Mathura, Ujjain, Dwarka and Kanchipuram. There is a Sanskrit shloka that goes:

'Kashi, Kanchi, Maya, Ayodhya, Avantika

Mathura, Dwaravati chaiva saptaita mokshadayika.'

(Varanasi, Kanchipuram, Haridwar, Ayodhya, Ujjain, Mathura, Dwarka are the seven cities that offer the liberation of moksha.)

The other great pilgrim trails are the two Char Dhams. The ancient one covers the subcontinent with the four *dhams* at Badrinath in the north in Uttarakhand; Dwarka in the west in Gujarat; Puri in the east in Odisha and Rameswaram in the south in Tamil Nadu. A smaller Char Dham yatra of Kedarnath, Badrinath, Gangotri and Yamunotri is in the Himalayas. In the past, rows and rows of pilgrims bent over their walking sticks would trek up stony hill paths, through pine forests and up glaciers to reach these tirthas. They were the true adventurers of our land.

LET'S GO SOME MORE!

This section is a sort of mishmash of the history of Indian people that I liked reading about and thought maybe you would enjoy it too. Here we have the story of the artists in prehistoric India, the merchants of an ancient port that vanished, a poet who also knew classical dance, and a tribe of legendary warriors who fought in the world wars.

THE ARTISTS OF BHIMBETKA

Imagine living over ten thousand years ago and wanting to become an artist. How would you draw or paint if you did not have paper, canvas, brushes or pencils? No problem, you made your paint and brushes yourself and painted on rocks!

- In 1957, archaeologist V.S. Wakankar discovered the caves of Bhimbetka in Madhya Pradesh, where hunter-gatherers had lived in prehistoric times, centuries before the Indus Valley Civilization.

- They excavated inside 700 caves and found stone tools that showed that people had lived here for thousands of years.

- What was amazing was that 400 caves had walls and ceilings covered in a dazzling array of colourful paintings, which author Devika Cariapa calls 'the world's largest open-air prehistoric art gallery'! Today, Bhimbetka is a UNESCO World Heritage site.

- The paint was analysed and scientists think the paintings were done during the Mesolithic period of 10,000 BCE. That is roughly 12,000 years ago.

- The paintings show scenes from everyday life. There are sticklike figures of men going hunting, carrying spears and bows and arrows. In some paintings, they are chasing wild animals and in others, the animals are chasing them!

- We see women cooking, children playing and the most beautiful are the paintings of people dancing. In the centre is a man wearing a tall, feathered headdress and playing a big drum. Around him, there are rows of dancers moving, holding hands and you can easily imagine them swaying to the beat of the drum.

- Archaeologists have counted twenty-nine species of animals, including deer, boar, tiger, lion, bison, elephant, rhinoceros and also fish and crocodiles. There are many jumping monkeys too. You also see dogs accompanying the men, so they must have been pets.

- It must have been pretty scary facing a tiger or a boar with just a bow and arrow, especially since the animals are often drawn larger than the hunters. In some scenes, the men are shown running away from charging animals.

- The artists used a wide palette of sixteen colours that have lasted till today. How did they make black, white, red, green, yellow, orange and even purple? They ground rocks and minerals, dried leaves, flowers and vegetable roots. They made brushes with twigs and animal fur.

- Since the discovery of Bhimbetka, over twenty more sites of rock paintings have been found, from the Edakkal Caves in Kerala to Burzahom in Kashmir. So the hunter-gatherers had spread all across India.

- It is amazing how cave art has a very similar style of painting and you can see these works in Altamira, Spain; Lascaux, France; Tadrart Acacus, Libya; Namadgi, Australia; Magura, Bulgaria; and Yunnan in China. All of them show hunters, animals and dancers.

- The art of the cave painters has survived for so long. Even today, tribal communities like the Warlis, Bhils, Gonds and

Rathwars paint the walls of their homes with rows of stick figures all dancing together.

- The paintings are like an ancient comic strip with people moving, dancing, aiming a spear or bow, running and playing. They wear a dhoti, jewellery and headgear. In some places you see palm prints, like we do in art class and some of the prints are so small they must have been children dipping their hands into paint and slapping them on the walls of the caves, saying, 'Look! I am here!'

THE MERCHANTS OF MUZIRIS

It is one of the mysteries of history that archaeologists are trying to solve. Muziris was a famous port on the Malabar Coast of Kerala that vanished one day. And no one knows where it had stood.

- A shipping guide written in the 1st century CE by an anonymous Greek sailor called *Periplus of the Erythraean Sea* or a Guide to the Ports of the Arabian Sea, lists many Indian ports and one of them he calls Muziris.

- A 2nd century CE map called *Tabula Peutingeriana* or Pentinger's Map also shows Muziris and near it a Roman temple of Augustus. From that, we can guess that Roman merchants were living in Muziris and even built a temple.

- Muziris stood by the banks of the Periyar River and ships would anchor out at sea. The goods from Europe were unloaded into boats and brought to port by local guides. Then the goods from India, like pepper, spices and cotton textiles were taken by boats to be loaded on the ships.

- Ships came from Arabia, Africa and the Gulf region and crossed the Arabian Sea with the help of the monsoon winds that filled the sails. These winds arrived like clockwork, moving east in summer and west in winter. It was the Arab sailors who had discovered the power of the monsoons.

- India's biggest market was the Roman Empire. There was also trade with China and the islands of Indonesia like Java and Bali. Hoards of Roman gold coins have been found along the Malabar Coast, showing how big the trade was.

- So Muziris was a cosmopolitan city where people speaking many languages were wandering in the bazaars. There were Romans, Greeks, Egyptians, Ethiopians, Arabs, Persians and Chinese. We called them all 'yavanas', the Sanskrit word for Greeks.

- The Roman writer Pliny described Muziris as the 'first emporium of India' and even warned of river pirates. Of course, Pliny was not happy with the money Romans were spending buying Indian goods like expensive textiles and spices.

- A Tamil poem, Purananuru, describes Muciri, 'With its streets, its houses, its covered fishing boats, where they sell fish, where they pile up rice. With the shifting and mingling crowds of a boisterous riverbank. Where the sacks of pepper are heaped up . . .' Even today, if you wander around the port of Kochi, you will see the shops selling an amazing selection of spices, especially piles of green and black pepper, as the fishing boats head out to sea.

- In 2007, a pile of broken Roman crockery was found near the village of Pattanam near the town of Kodungallur, in the Thrissur district in Kerala. Three archaeologists of the Kerala Council for Historical Research began to excavate.

- They have found Roman jars called amphorae used to store
  wine and olive oil; glass and semi-precious stone beads for
  jewellery; blue-and-white tableware from China; Persian
  tiles; and Arab jars. The Roman coins found here are from
  the reigns of the emperors Augustus and Tiberius.

- They have also unearthed a brick wharf where the boats must
  have landed and in the river mud, the fossilized remains of
  a six-foot canoe.

- According to the Syrian Christian community, St Thomas,
  a disciple of Jesus Christ, landed at Muziris and
  introduced Christianity to Kerala.

- So how could such a busy and prosperous port vanish? Historians think that in 1341 CE, there was a severe cyclone and the land was flooded—Muziris never recovered. Just like they think the port of Kaveripattinam on the Cholamandalam Coast may have been swept away by a tsunami.

A POET FOR DANCERS

We know of Bhakti poets like Tukaram, Mirabai and Guru Nanak, whose poetry is set to music and sung by devotees. What makes the Bhakti poet Srimanta Sankardev of Assam so special?

- Sankardev (born 1449) was not just a poet but also a scholar and playwright, a social and religious reformer. He also inspired a classical dance called Sattriya. It was declared a classical dance by the Sangeet Natak Akademi in 2000.

- Sankardev established monasteries and community centres called *sattras*. Here, monks lived and people came to pray at the temple.

- The first sattra was established in Majuli, which is an island in the mighty Brahmaputra River. In 2016, it was declared the largest river island in the world.

- Sankardev was a wanderer and travelled across India for twelve years, visiting places sacred to Lord Krishna like Mathura, Vrindavan, Dwarka and Puri.

- Most of his poetry is in praise of Krishna and, once set to music, is called *borgeet*. He composed his first borgeet in Badrinath. This song is in a surprising mix of two languages—Assamese and Maithili, which is spoken in Bihar.

- He wrote dance dramas called *ankia naat* and as the dances were performed by the monks at the sattras, the dance form was called Sattriya.

- Every sattra has a prayer hall called *namghar* and the monks perform here, but not before an image of Krishna. Instead, a copy of the Bhagavata Purana, which tells the story of Krishna, is placed in the eastern corner.

WARRIORS FROM THE HILLS

In the emerald green forested and hilly landscape of Nagaland live some of the most colourful tribes of our land—the Nagas. For centuries they have grown rice, woven brilliantly coloured shawls and the men have often gone to war. Meet the warrior dancers of Nagaland.

- The Naga tribes speak over eighty different dialects and sometimes they are so different, people can't understand each other! So the government of Nagaland declared English the official language.

- Among the various tribes are the Angami, Ao, Anal, Konyak and Rengma. The men were very proud of being hunters and warriors and so they were often at war with each other and in the past, they were also headhunters!

- The Nagas living very isolated lives in the hills knew little about the outside world. They had some contact with the Ahom kings of Assam, but it was only with the arrival of Christian missionaries from the United States in the 19th century that they learnt of the rest of the world.

- We know that Sikh soldiers from Punjab fought in the two world wars—so did the Nagas. 2000 Naga soldiers took part in the First World War in Europe. During the Second World War when Japan invaded the region and captured Kohima, Naga soldiers were part of the Allied forces and as they knew the region, they acted as guides for the British army.

- Ursula Graham Bower (1914–88) was a British anthropologist who lived among the Nagas for many years to study their lives. During the Second World War, she led a team of 150 Naga warriors through the jungles to fight the Japanese. She also helped refugees who were escaping from Myanmar. Bower was a very good shot and used a Sten gun.

- The Nagas enjoy dancing and rows of male Naga dancers, clad in black-and-red costumes, covered in jewellery and tattoos, their tall headdresses swaying, are a magnificent sight.

- Take a close look at the dancers as they stamp their feet, wave their spears and yell their battle cries. The headdress is topped by the feathers of the hornbill bird and decorated with the canine teeth of wild boars.

- The shawls woven by women in black, red and blue are famous. Both men and women wear a lot of jewellery made of beads, glass, stone, shell, metals, animal tusks, horns and even fur.

- In 2000, the Government of Nagaland began a yearly celebration called the Hornbill Festival, named after the colourful bird with the huge curved beak. The idea was to gather the tribes for a celebration and help them learn about each other in a friendly ambience.

- At the festivals, the tribes stay in wooden houses that are designed in the tradition of each tribe. They cook their food and dance and sing. So tribes who had once fought with each other met, sang and danced together, shared their food and discovered they had much in common. Every year they also get the opportunity to meet people from other parts of India.

- Soon Hornbill was being called the 'Festival of Festivals' and every January, tourists visit Kohima by the thousands. The most popular show is the International Rock Concert, where bands play every night, filling the air with guitar riffs and drum rhythms; the audience joins in with dancing and stomping feet. It is a truly great show! Naga style!

~~~~~~

The Many Things We Can Do With History

I agree history books can be scary. They scare me too. They are usually very fat and then they are written in this grim, gloomy way. Often, they are full of long paragraphs, footnotes and bibliographies that make you think you are drowning in words, facts, names and dates. So who wants to read history books anyway?

The real problem is that when the history of India stretches to nearly five thousand years, the books get bigger. But you don't have to remember it all! No way!

If you don't read history books, you are missing something. They are often full of stories because, think about it, the word 'history' has the word 'story' hidden in it. It is our story, about our lives. Once you get past your nervousness and open a history book, you will discover it is about people and events that make for fascinating stories. They can be very, very different from textbooks and are not so obsessed with dates, kings and battles. They have stories about people.

Here are a few clever ways to get to the interesting bits and discover all the fascinating things about our past without getting in a funk. Besides, everything has a history, from sports and science to fashions and food. So maybe you can start with the history of cricket or the history of Indian cuisines.

BOOKS TO READ

Below is a short list of some of the books that I used while writing this book. I am not asking you to read all of them, honest! But if you are looking for information on any aspect of India's past from events and battles to poetry, science and even food, these books have them. Just look up the topic in the index at the back and zip to the page where you'll find it. Easy peasy!

1. *The Wonder That Was India* by A.L. Basham (Rupa, 1981)

2. *India, a History* by John Keay (HarperCollins, 2010)

3. *An Advanced History of India* by R.C. Majumdar, Kalikinkar Datta and H.C. Raychaudhuri (Macmillan, 2011)

4. *A History of South India* by K.A. Nilakanta Sastri (Oxford University Press, 1997)

5. *Daily Life in Ancient India* by Jeannine Auboyer (Munshiram Manoharlal, 1994)

6. *Indian Food: A Historical Companion* by K.T. Achaya (Oxford University Press, 1998)

7. *The First Spring* by Abraham Eraly (Viking)

8. *The Last Spring* by Abraham Eraly (Viking)

9. *A Children's History of India* by Subhadra Sen Gupta (Rupa, 2015)

10. *The Penguin Dictionary of Indian Classical Music* by Raghava R. Menon (Penguin, 1995)

ENTER THE INTERNET

You don't have to read books all the time anyway. Remember, there is the internet! The best way to get information really quickly. There is a lot of information on the internet though, so you should be careful—it is not always correct. Start with Google. Go to www.google.com and type the subject you are looking for. Check the websites of uuniversities and encyclopaedias, these are usually quite reliable. It is fun wandering around the internet and discovering weird information about famous people, and it will also improve your class projects.

LONG WALKS AND MUSEUM VISITS

History really comes alive if you visit a monument. In India, old buildings are everywhere. Touch the carvings on the pillars of a temple or walk on marble floors of palaces and the past comes alive. Museums are stuffed with the things people used in the past—pots and pans, clothes and coins, swords and daggers. Most museums are huge, so don't try to see it all in one day, or your head will begin to buzz. Pick a period, like the Indus Valley Civilization or the Cholas, and just wander around letting the sculptures and paintings talk to you. My favourite galleries at the National Museum in Delhi are the one on the Indus Valley

Civilization and another called Arms and Armour, with truly amazing swords, daggers and guns.

History is everywhere. Read books on history, watch historical films and television serials and you'll discover the lives of the people of the past and their stories that make history so fascinating. Then talk to your parents and grandparents and discover the history of your family and make a family tree. That is history too!

Let's Go
TIME TRAVELLING!
LIFE IN INDIA THROUGH THE AGES
SUBHADRA SEN GUPTA
Illustrated by Tapas Guha

Go time travelling through the alleys of history and take a tour through the various ages, from Harappa to the Maurayan, Mughal to the British with *Let's Go Time Travelling!*

Read More in Puffin by Subhadra Sen Gupta

The Constitution of India for Children

Every 26th January, people gather on New Delhi's Rajpath amidst a colourful jamboree of fluttering flags, marching soldiers and dancing children. What is celebrated on this day is at the heart of our democracy—the magnificent Constitution of India.

The document didn't only lay down the law but united India with a vision that took two years, eleven months and seventeen days to realise. Subhadra Sen Gupta captures the many momentous occasions in Indian history that led to its making in *The Constitution of India for Children*. This book provides answers to innumerable questions asked over the years.

Which language is our Constitution written in?
Were women a part of the team that drafted the Constitution?
Why do political parties have symbols next to their names?
What is the official language of India?

An essential handbook for every student and denizen of India, here is a compendium of knowledge that serves as an insightful introduction to the most important document of Independent India.

Saffron, White and Green: The Amazing Story of India's Independence

It is one of the most exciting stories in history—the glorious tale of how the powerless, unarmed people of India came together to defy the mightiest empire in the world. The British empire had tightened its noose around a country split by religion, class and caste. But when the people rallied under the tricoloured banner of freedom, it was with a power that stunned even the strongest. No one had seen such a revolution before.

What was truly extraordinary was that India won her independence not through an armed uprising but by persistent, peaceful, non-violent protests. And a nation of millions held its breath proudly as Jawaharlal Nehru spoke of its tryst with destiny. Not long after, India inspired colonies across the world to stand up and demand independence.

This is the story of Ahimsa, satyagraha and Swaraj, of non-violence and the struggle for truth—all for the one thing that is most valuable to a people and to a nation: freedom.